л ⊂4

New

D0559156

Mac OS X Snow Leopard
Pocket Guide

Mac OS X Snow Leopard
Pocket Guide

Chris Seibold

O'REILLY®

Beijing · Cambridge · Farnham · Köln · Sebastopol · Taipei · Tokyo

Mac OS X Snow Leopard Pocket Guide
by Chris Seibold

Copyright © 2009 Chris Seibold. All rights reserved.
Printed in Canada.

Published by O'Reilly Media, Inc., 1005 Gravenstein Highway North, Sebastopol, CA 95472.

O'Reilly books may be purchased for educational, business, or sales promotional use. Online editions are also available for most titles (*http://my.safari booksonline.com*). For more information, contact our corporate/institutional sales department: 800-998-9938 or *corporate@oreilly.com*.

Editors: Simon St.Laurent and Brian Jepson
Production Editor: Loranah Dimant
Production Services: Appingo, Inc.
Indexer: Ellen Troutman Zaig
Cover Designer: Karen Montgomery
Interior Designer: David Futato
Illustrator: Robert Romano

Printing History:
September 2009:   First Edition.

ISBN: 978-0-596-80272-1

[TM]

1252089198

Contents

Preface   vii

Chapter 1: What's New in Snow Leopard?   1
   Grand Central Dispatch   2
   True 64-bit Operating System   3
   Microsoft Exchange Support   4
   OpenCL   4
   Smoking JavaScript   5
   Smaller Footprint   5
   Application and Finder Enhancements   6
   System Improvements   11
   Snow Leopard Offers Even More   12

Chapter 2: Installing Snow Leopard and Migrating Data   13
   Which Macs Are Compatible?   13
   Preparing to Install Snow Leopard   15

Chapter 3: The Quick Guide to Snow Leopard   31
   What You Need To Know About Mac OS X   31
   Using Snow Leopard   38
   Snow Leopard Basics   42
   Standard Window Controls   79

Files and Folders   81
Nonessential But Useful Mac OS X Features   84

Chapter 4: Quick Guide to Troubleshooting Mac OS X   99
Common Problems   99

Chapter 5: System Preferences   115
Preferences and Your Mac   115
Preference Pane Rundown   117
Non-Apple Preference Panes   154

Chapter 6: Built-in Applications and Utilities   157
Applications Installed with Snow Leopard   158
Utilities Included with Snow Leopard   174

Chapter 7: MobileMe   183
Back to My Mac   185
Adding or Removing a Computer to/from MobileMe   187
iDisk   187
Clearing the MobileMe Sync Slate   187

Chapter 8: Security   189
Password Management   190

Chapter 9: Keyboard Commands and Special Characters   195
Key Commands   195
Typing Special Characters in Mac OS X   202

Index   207

Preface

OS X was first released to the public a decade ago as Mac OS X Beta (code name Kodiak). The decade after the introduction saw Mac OS X go from interesting oddity unsuited to daily work to a usable operating system (OS) with little third-party support to everything most people want out of an operating system and a little more.

Apple will tell you that Leopard, the version of Mac OS X that preceded Snow Leopard, is a great OS. The point of Snow Leopard, Apple argues, isn't to improve on Leopard as much as it is to give developers a chance to take advantage of emerging technologies and to streamline Mac OS X. Snow Leopard features a lot of improvements for developers to love. Access to Grand Central promises to allow better use of the multicore CPUs that are now standard on all Macs, Open CL offers developers a way to harness the ever-growing power of video cards, and the omission of support for the PowerPC architecture allows Apple to deliver a leaner installation.

There is a lot more to Snow Leopard than goodies for the developers and an internal polishing by Apple. Snow Leopard doesn't feature any eye-popping, must-have new features, but there are enough enhancements scattered throughout Snow Leopard that any Mac user with an Intel machine will appreciate the upgrade.

What kind of enhancements can you expect? Everything is faster. Sometimes you'll notice the speedup (such as the speed with which it starts up, shuts down, and sleeps), and sometimes you won't. You can also expect some very nice application upgrades. iChat uses less bandwidth and features a bigger window when you are in a video chat. Preview offers new options for editing images. The Dock gets an upgrade, incorporating Exposé into each application's icon. QuickTime has become Quicktime X and offers you a new way to add videos to your MobileMe or YouTube account.

That is just a sampling of the upgrades in Snow Leopard. Taken individually, they aren't that big of a deal; when you look at all the small improvements, they add up to a substantial update to Mac OS X.

Conventions Used in This Book

The following typographical conventions are used in this book:

Italic

> Indicates new terms, URLs, email addresses, filenames, and file extensions.

`Constant width bold`

> Shows commands or other text that should be typed literally by the user.

`Constant width italic`

> Shows text that should be replaced with user-supplied values or by values determined by context.

Menu Symbols

If you use *Mac OS Snow Leopard Pocket Guide* exclusively, you'll always know which button to press. The key that reads "option" is called Option throughout the book. The key with the clover symbol (officially called the "Places of Interest" symbol) is represented by ⌘, which looks precisely like the symbol on the keyboard (older Apple keyboards also feature the Apple logo). Apple itself uses some symbols for these keys that you won't see on the keyboard. If you click the menu bar, you'll see symbols next to some commands that indicate the keyboard shortcut you can use. For example, if you click the Edit menu from within the TextEdit program, you'll see a long sequence of symbols for the "Paste and Match Style" shortcut, as shown in Figure P-1.

Figure P-1. Keyboard shortcuts shown in the Edit menu

From left to right, the symbols to the right of "Paste and Match Style" and the left of V are: Option (the left-tilting stylized symbol), Shift (the up arrow), and Command (the ⌘ described earlier). This indicates that you need to hold down Option-Shift-⌘ while pressing V. You'd see this as Option-Shift-⌘-V in this book.

A less commonly used modifier is the Control key, which Apple symbolizes with the ^ symbol. This book spells it out as "Control." You may also encounter a broken circle with an arrow pointing to the upper-left, which indicates esc (escape).

The symbol for the Eject button is the same as the symbol that is silk-screened onto most Apple keyboards (a solid arrow pointing up with a single line below it). The Delete key is symbolized with ⌫.

Using Code Examples

This book is here to help you get your job done. In general, you may use the code in this book in your programs and documentation. You do not need to contact us for permission unless you're reproducing a significant portion of the code. For example, writing a program that uses several chunks of code from this book does not require permission. Selling or distributing a CD-ROM of examples from O'Reilly books does require permission. Answering a question by citing this book and quoting example code does not require permission. Incorporating a significant amount of example code from this book into your product's documentation does require permission.

We appreciate, but do not require, attribution. An attribution usually includes the title, author, publisher, and ISBN. For example: "*Mac OS X Snow Leopard Pocket Guide*, by Chris Seibold. Copyright 2009 Chris Seibold, 978-0-596-80272-1."

If you feel your use of code examples falls outside fair use or the permission given above, feel free to contact us at *permissions@oreilly.com*.

Safari® Books Online

 Safari Books Online is an on-demand digital library that lets you easily search over 7,500 technology and creative reference books and videos to find the answers you need quickly.

With a subscription, you can read any page and watch any video from our library online. Read books on your cell phone and mobile devices. Access new titles before they are available for print, and get exclusive access to manuscripts in development and post feedback for the authors. Copy and paste code samples, organize your favorites, download chapters, bookmark key sections, create notes, print out pages, and benefit from tons of other time-saving features.

O'Reilly Media has uploaded this book to the Safari Books Online service. To have full digital access to this book and others on similar topics from O'Reilly and other publishers, sign up for free at *http://my.safaribooksonline.com*.

How to Contact Us

Please address comments and questions concerning this book to the publisher:

> O'Reilly Media, Inc.
> 1005 Gravenstein Highway North
> Sebastopol, CA 95472
> 800-998-9938 (in the United States or Canada)
> 707-829-0515 (international or local)
> 707 829-0104 (fax)

We have a web page for this book, where we list errata, examples, and additional information. You can access this page at:

> *http://www.oreilly.com/catalog/9780596802721*

To comment or ask technical questions about this book, send email to:

> *bookquestions@oreilly.com*

For more information about our books, conferences, Resource Centers, and the O'Reilly Network, see our website at:

> *http://www.oreilly.com*

Acknowledgments

On a personal note, I'd like to thank Hadley Stern for both doing the technical editing on *Mac OS X Snow Leopard Pocket Guide* and for introducing me to the world of writing books. I'd also like to thank Brian Jepson, who edited this book. If you ever feel the need to write a book, and the experience is quite rewarding, do whatever is in your power to get Brian Jepson on the team. Your book will be better for it and you'll be personally improved by the experience. Plus, that guy knows everything there is to know about computers (all varieties), hacking, pop culture, and philosophy. Even better, he can work all the topics into a single joke.

What's New in Snow Leopard?

In 2000 the first iteration of Mac OS X was released to the public. It was called, without much imagination, Mac OS X Public Beta. Users who were eager to get in on the future of Macintosh were able to pay $29 for the privilege of being beta testers.

A lot has changed since Mac OS X Public Beta was released. Most of the changes were predictable—faster processors and more RAM—but some weren't. One of the unpredictable changes was the switch to Intel processors. The switch to Intel left Apple supporting multiple chip architectures, a trick Apple managed with the addition of *Rosetta* for translating PowerPC instructions to Intel instructions for two versions of Mac OS X (Tiger and Leopard). Snow Leopard is the first version of Mac OS X to drop support for PowerPC-based Macs.

In Snow Leopard, Apple took the opportunity to further streamline the code behind the operating system. When you use Snow Leopard, you'll notice faster start ups, a smaller disk footprint for the OS, and an all-around snappier feel.

What you won't notice as immediately is all the effort Apple has put into making Snow Leopard a fully modern operating system. Apple has built-in support to take full advantage of today's multiple core chips, the power of graphics cards, and the ever-expanding amount of RAM available to today's computers. Snow Leopard isn't just a nice release for this particular moment in time; it is a forward-looking iteration of Mac OS X that paves an easy path to the future.

Grand Central Dispatch

For years chip developers fought a megahertz and gigahertz war. To improve the performance of processors, chip manufacturers worked ceaselessly to produce chips that ran at ever-higher frequencies. That strategy came with heavy costs. As the clock frequency increased, the chips demanded more electricity and produced more heat. A really hot, power-hungry processor isn't the most desirable solution for better performance, particularly if it is being used in a notebook.

The solution chip manufacturers created was multiple processing cores on the same chip. The idea being that by sandwiching two or more cores on a single chip, computers would effectively have multiple CPUs, thereby dramatically increasing performance.

The idea of adding more chips or cores to increase performance isn't new; Apple was selling a multiple CPU system in 1997. The problem that multiple chip or multicore computers have faced isn't one of raw computing power, but rather one of actually using all the computing power available to the machine. In days gone by, only programs specifically written for multiple processor machines could take advantage of multiple cores or chips. That kind of programming can be difficult to do, so developers often don't take the time to make their programs multicore aware.

Grand Central Dispatch (GCD) addresses the problem of multiple processor usage by taking the hard work out of programming for multiple core systems. Instead, developers can program to make their applications GCD-capable. If a program is GCD-enabled, Snow Leopard will take care of the onerous chore of distributing processing tasks across the available cores.

The upshot for the end user is many more multicore-aware programs and a faster computing experience throughout the system. You'll never know that Grand Central Dispatch is working behind the scenes to balance the loads between cores, but you'll notice the bump in speed as more and more applications are able to efficiently use all the cores in your Mac.

True 64-bit Operating System

Chips aren't just getting more cores, they're also getting more bits. 64-bit computing isn't new, but it was traditionally reserved for research settings and tech-heavy places where serious computing was going on. Now that 64-bit chips are available to anyone looking to buy a Mac, it would be an obvious waste of the chip's capabilities if they were saddled with a 32-bit system.

Why is the computer world heading to 64-bits? One big reason is the amount of memory computers can routinely hold. A Mac Pro can hold up to 32 GB, but 32-bit applications can't use all 32 GB; 32-bit applications can only address 4 GB of physical RAM. 64-bit applications can address (in theory) up to 16 billion GB.

In Snow Leopard, Mac OS X can now boot into a 64-bit kernel on certain systems (hold the 6 and 4 key down while booting). Even if you don't boot into the 64-bit kernel, many of Snow Leopard's built-in applications are 64-bit and run happily under the 32-bit kernel.

A 64-bit system isn't just useful for the amount of memory it can address. With the 64-bit enhancements in Snow Leopard, applications benefit from hardware-assisted technologies to protect against malicious software.

In Snow Leopard, Apple has rewritten every application except Grapher, iTunes, DVD Player, and Front Row as 64-bit applications. So Safari, for example, can address more memory in your Mac and benefits from the security features as well. This means a faster, more secure computing experience when you're using any of the updated applications.

Microsoft Exchange Support

If you work in a corporate environment, there is a good chance you use Microsoft Exchange. Microsoft Exchange is the extremely popular email server and collaboration service. Snow Leopard features out-of-the-box support for Microsoft Exchange 2007 servers. If your computing environment includes contacts, email, and calendars served up by Microsoft Exchange 2007, you'll be able to stay up to date.

OpenCL

Any Mac that can run Snow Leopard (except for the older, single-core Mac Mini) has multiple cores, hence the usefulness of Grand Central Dispatch. But the CPUs aren't the only source of number crunching available to your Mac. Your Mac also has a video card. The video is built into the core chipset on some models; on other models, video is handled by a separate, dedicated card known as the Graphics Processing Unit (GPU). Since that card holds a lot of independent computing power, particularly suited to certain types of computational challenges, it would be great if there was a way to tap the power for something other than the moments your Mac needs all that horsepower for gaming or rendering.

Open Computing Language, or Open CL, is Apple's effort to squeeze maximum performance out of the hardware available. Developers will be able to tap the potential of video cards to aid your Mac with its processing duties. If you're discounting the amount of power contained in a GPU, consider that the University of Antwerp created a supercomputer out of eight graphics cards. Even a single graphic card, if fed the right kind of processing problems, can significantly add to your Mac's overall computing power.

After reading that, you might think if you run out and buy a Mac Pro with four video cards, it would provide you with unparalleled speed (it's a top end Mac plus half a super computer, right?) but, at least for now, the payoff won't be as big as you might expect. The kind of tasks that GPUs excel at aren't the same that CPUs excel at processing. Consider this a bit of future-proofing: as the power of GPUs grow, developers will be able to take advantage of that power.

Smoking JavaScript

Most people never give a second thought to programming languages in general, and definitely don't spend a lot of time thinking about a particular programming language. The Safari team isn't most people, and they have spent a lot of time thinking about a specific programming language—JavaScript.

Why be obsessed with JavaScript and not, say, Pascal? Because JavaScript is all over the Web. JavaScript is part of the power behind AJAX (Asynchronous JavaScript and XML) and DHTML (Dynamic Hyper Text Markup Language). When you use a website that responds like a regular desktop application, there is a good chance that JavaScript is involved. Since it is such a web workhorse, speeding up JavaScript makes your browsing experience much better and the version of Safari bundled with Snow Leopard speeds up JavaScript substantially. Safari also includes some interesting enhancements, such as support for hardware-accelerated 3D operations right in the web browser.

Smaller Footprint

Mac OS X is slimming down. A Snow Leopard install takes less space than a Leopard install. How much less space? Well, that depends on how you configure the installation of Snow Leopard (if you choose to configure it at all). The smallest install of Snow Leopard requires a mere 8 GB of space, whereas using everything on the install disk version requires 11.6 GB of space. If you upgrade from Leopard to Snow Leopard, chances are you'll find that up to 6 GB of disk space have been freed up.

Where did the space savings come from? Has Mac OS X been stripped of functionality to free up a little hard drive space? Thankfully, no. Remember that one key bit of functionality has been removed: support for the PowerPC platform. Previous versions of Mac OS X combined the software for Intel and PowerPC platforms into one big file. With the PowerPC support gone, these files are much smaller.

NOTE

Rosetta, the technology that lets you run old PowerPC applications on Intel-based Macs, is still in there. So if you've got some old applications you need to keep running, you're still in luck.

Application and Finder Enhancements

The lion's share of the changes in Snow Leopard are more esoteric than most users are accustomed to, but that doesn't mean there aren't plenty of changes at an application level. Apple may have had all the company's focus trained on the stuff that runs the applications you love to use, but a good bit of innovation and newness managed to slip into the applications as well. The changes, and how they affect what you do with Mac OS X, are explored more completely in the appropriate chapters, but you can get a quick overview by reading the rest of this chapter.

Finder Enhancements

What program do most Mac OS X users use more often than any other? The Finder. When you're browsing through files or opening applications, you are using the Finder. The good news is that the Finder has been upgraded. It is faster in Snow

Leopard (the Finder takes advantage of the underlying 64-bit nature of Snow Leopard and the multicore power of Grand Central Dispatch). But the Finder isn't just speedier, the application also sports some new features. There are enough changes in the Finder to justify the $29 upgrade price of Snow Leopard, so a quick list of the biggest stuff will let you know what to look for. If you're after more information on what has changed, Chapter 2 will reveal how to utilize the new features.

Better icons

The icons in Snow Leopard are bigger; they scale all the way up to 512×512 pixels. The initial reaction to icon sizes that large is one of befuddlement: what could be the point of such a large icon? A folder at 512×512 doesn't reveal any more information than a folder represented at some arbitrary lesser resolution. In Snow Leopard, the large icon sizes are actually very useful. Look at a text document's icon and you can actually read the text. Look at a spreadsheet and you'll get a glimpse of the columns of numbers. If you're rolling through your video folder, you can watch an entire movie in icon view.

More control over the sidebar

The sidebar made its debut with Leopard and provided a way to get at often-used folders, servers, disks, and devices. Useful but a bit cluttered if you didn't take advantage of everything the sidebar offered. With Snow Leopard, the sidebar is more malleable. You can still add searches and the like, but now you can also delete the headers you don't want to use. The change doesn't have to be permanent— the moment you want the deleted header back, just drag the item to the sidebar and it will reappear.

The Finder can put that back for you

If you've done a bit of housekeeping on your Mac and have a Trash can full of items, you might decide you want to keep some of them after all. But where did that file in the Trash come from in the first place? In Snow Leopard, you won't have to guess, because the Finder can put it back (right-click or Control-click on a file in the Trash, and select Put Back).

Application Enhancements

The Finder isn't the only application in Snow Leopard to get upgraded. Almost every application has been rewritten for 64-bit compatibility. Some applications received more than just a new version number; they also received some improvements in performance or usability.

iChat

iChat is the video/audio/text chatting application built-in to Mac OS X. iChat has always been easy to use, but in Snow Leopard it has been significantly improved:

Better connectivity

Some iChat users were stymied by connectivity issues when using video chat. The reason didn't have anything to do with the Mac, it had to do with servers and compatibility. iChat addresses these problems in Snow Leopard by fixing the incompatibilities or, if the problem can't be resolved, by routing the chat through an AIM (AOL Instant Message) server. That video chat that didn't work before will work now!

See more with iChat

In Snow Leopard, maximum resolution of a chat has been bumped up to 640×480 pixels. Apple calls that a 400% increase in resolution; to you it means more detail in your chat videos.

Less bandwidth

You're laughing at the increased resolution because you're worried about bandwidth? Part of the reason you can have such a huge chat window is because iChat under Snow Leopard uses much less bandwidth. A maximum resolution chat in Leopard requires almost a megabit of bandwidth to your ISP (900 Kbps to be exact), whereas iChat under Snow Leopard requires only one-third of that to achieve maximum quality.

Different statuses for every account

You probably have more than one iChat account. Perhaps you have one for work and one for personal use. With Leopard, all your accounts got the same status messages. If you wanted "Drinking beer, feel free to ring me" on your personal account, while tossing up "Working diligently on Chapter 2" on your work account, you were out of luck. In the latest version of iChat, you can pull that trick off. Just don't give both iChat handles to your boss!

Quick Look enabled

People use iChat to swap files all the time; it is a convenient way of real-time file transfer, since you know immediately whether the file got to its destination. If you are on the receiving end of a transfer, you don't have to open the file to get a look at what is inside anymore; you can use Quick Look to see an instant preview.

Preview

Preview started out life as a way to view PDFs. Not very exciting, but through the various iterations of Preview, the application became much more than just a PDF viewer. Preview will do everything from image retouching to scanning. The version of Preview that ships with Snow Leopard offers some substantial improvements:

Better text selection

If you've ever tried to copy text from a multicolumn PDF document you know it can be a hassle. The text isn't selected in a rational manner. Preview fixes that. In the latest version, instead of selecting across columns when you don't want to, you can actually just select the paragraphs, or parts of a paragraph, you want.

Improved scaling

Preview has been able to zoom and scale images and documents for quite some time. But the results of the scaling weren't always ideal. Preview in Snow Leopard improves this behavior by using a new algorithm that decreases the annoying artifacts that bothered sharp-eyed users.

Annotations just got much easier

You could annotate PDFs and images with earlier versions of Preview, but the latest version makes it much easier. The version of Preview with Snow Leopard includes an annotation toolbar. Any time you want to make a note, click the Toolbar and point out the great (or horrible) stuff on a PDF.

Image correction histogram

In Leopard, Preview's ability to correct images gained some improvements. In Snow Leopard, you get a live RGB histogram view for your image, which you can use to adjust color just like in iPhoto.

Import from scanner

Got a scanner but hate the bundled software? Don't use it. You can now scan images directly into Preview and change them (or save them to edit in a different program).

QuickTime X

One application that got a lot of attention in Snow Leopard is QuickTime. More than just a new version number, QuickTime got a new name: QuickTime X. What's new in QuickTime X?

QuickTime player

When you open a file with QuickTime, you won't see the player you were expecting. Apple has reworked Quick-Time player to make the controls invisible except for the moments you need them. If you've played a video with QuickTime in full screen, you have a good idea of what the new player looks like.

Capture media

Want to create a quick video of yourself? Of your screen? No problem in the new QuickTime. You can capture a video using your Mac's built-in iSight or attached camera and post it directly to MobileMe or YouTube. Even better?

When you're posting the videos you make, you won't have to worry about choosing the right codec or resolution, QuickTime X will take care of that drudgery for you.

Trim media

Is that video too long? Cut a few seconds off in QuickTime with the new media clip trimming capabilities.

Chapters with images

If you are viewing a multichapter video such as a DVD, you won't be stuck with the often unrevealing chapter names when trying to navigate. QuickTime provides you with a thumbnail of a frame from the chapter to help you decide where you want to jump to next.

System Improvements

Some of the improvements in Snow Leopard are system-wide. These improvements are there without regard to the particular application you're using and, in some cases, even when you're not using any applications at all.

Faster Wake Up, Faster Shut Down, Faster Wireless Network Logon

No one likes waiting on their computer to do something. Snow Leopard decreases waiting and increases productivity. Joining a wireless network is faster using Snow Leopard, which is a nice bonus when you change hot spots frequently. If you put your Mac to sleep when you're not using it, you'll be happy to know that your Mac will wake even faster from sleep than it did when you were using an older version of Mac OS X. You'll also appreciate the difference when you shut down, as Snow Leopard is noticeably faster when the shutdown sequence is invoked.

Split Pane Terminal

The Terminal in Mac OS X is either something you never use or something you use all the time. If you use the Terminal all the time, you'll be pleased with the new split pane Terminal window.

Gamma Settings

Snow Leopard changes the default Gamma correction from 1.8 to 2.2. For some users, the change is purely esoteric; for users who work with color often, the change is substantial.

Snow Leopard Offers Even More

There's more to Snow Leopard than what is listed here. You'll find new niceties every time you use Snow Leopard. Some changes are subtle, some are minor; but taken together, the improvements in Snow Leopard add up to a more productive and pleasant experience.

CHAPTER 2

Installing Snow Leopard and Migrating Data

New Macs come with Snow Leopard (10.6) preinstalled, but if you're running Leopard or earlier, you'll need to install Snow Leopard before you can have fun with it. Even if you bought a new Mac yesterday with Snow Leopard preinstalled, you may need to move data from your old Mac to your new Mac. If you fit into either of these categories, this chapter is for you.

Which Macs Are Compatible?

Snow Leopard is compatible with all Intel-based Macs. If your Mac is one of the following (or newer), you can run Snow Leopard. There are a few other requirements: 1 GB of RAM (early MacBook Pros and Mini might not have it) and 5 GB of disk space.

- Mac Mini (early 2006 and later)
- MacBook (all models)
- Mac Pro (all models)
- iMac (early 2006 and later)
- Xserve (late 2006)
- MacBook Pro (all models)

- MacBook Air (all models)

What determines which Mac makes the cut? The processor. Snow Leopard is Intel-only, so any Mac that relies on a PowerPC processor can't run Snow Leopard. If you're wondering whether your Mac is Intel- or PowerPC-based, a quick trip to the Apple menu will resolve the issue. Click the Apple in the upper-lefthand corner of the screen and select About This Mac. The information is next to the entry for Processor as shown in Figure 2-1.

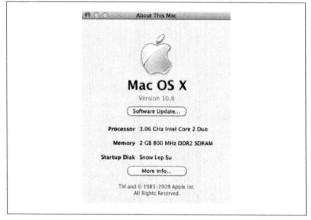

Figure 2-1. If your Mac says Intel, you are ready to go

Compatibility isn't the entire story with Snow Leopard. Depending on which Intel Mac you have, you may be able to run a 64-bit kernel. In Leopard, and on most Macs running Snow Leopard, Mac OS X runs a 32-bit kernel that can run both 32-bit and 64-bit applications. On supported machines, Snow Leopard expands the 64-bit support to include the kernel (although with some exceptions, like Xserves, the 64-bit kernel is not used by default). In normal use you wouldn't be able to tell the difference between a 32-bit and 64-bit kernel, but the 64-bit kernel will be able to (in theory) address up to 16 terabytes of RAM. Compare that to the 32-bit kernel, which can natively address up to 64 GB (as of this writing, Mac Pros top out at 32 GB) of RAM thanks to the Physical Address Extension (PAE) of Intel chips, which effectively extends the address space to 36 bits. However, even with PAE, individual 32-bit applications were limited to 4 GB of RAM. With 64-bits applications, the 4 GB limit is removed.

Preparing to Install Snow Leopard

Once you are sure your Mac is up to the task of running Snow Leopard, it is time to think about installation. To install Snow Leopard, you're going to have to boot from the installer disk. If you pop in the installer disk while you are running Leopard, you can double-click Install OS X and everything will be taken care of for you. You can also boot directly from the DVD by inserting it in the optical drive and restarting while holding ⌘-C, which forces your Mac to start from the optical drive. After you boot from the DVD, the first question you will be asked by the installer is what language you wish to use for the rest of the installation. This choice is a little more far reaching than it first appears; when you select a language for installation it becomes the default language for your Mac and also for the installer. To change the default language at a later time, you'll need to visit the Language & Text preference pane (see "Language & Text" on page 123).

After you choose the language, the installer will report that it is preparing the installation, and then you'll be presented with a welcome page. Clicking Continue brings up a license for you to Agree to (clicking Disagree, even if due to firmly reasoned principles, cancels the installation).

Once you've agreed to the terms of the software license agreement, a window opens revealing all your options for the installation destination. Snow Leopard isn't picky, so you aren't restricted to only internal drives; any Mac-formatted drive of sufficient space will be available, including FireWire and USB drives. Click the drive you want to install Snow Leopard on and you're ready to go.

NOTE

Snow Leopard can be installed on any drive that is formatted with Apple's Journaled HFS+ filesystem. You can run Disk Utility from the installer's Utilities menu to format or inspect the drives on your system.

Preparing Your Hard Disk

Previous versions of Mac OS X offered several options:

Install
> Upgrade or reinstall an existing installation or install Mac OS X on a pristine system.

Erase and Install
> Erase the hard drive and install Mac OS X.

Archive and Install
> Move your settings and System folder out of the way, and upgrade or reinstall Mac OS X.

With Snow Leopard, you get one choice: Install.

This is convenient as it requires no thinking on your part, but you might miss some of the older install options. The good news is that while the older options aren't explicit, you can still fake it.

If you'd like to duplicate the functionality of Erase and Install, you'll find the solution under the Utilities menu. Clicking on Utilities will reveal a drop-down menu with a bevy of useful utilities. If you'd like to erase your disk, run Disk Utility and you're ready to perform a home-brew version of Erase and Install.

WARNING

Exercise extreme caution when using Disk Utility and erasing drives. Make sure you're targeting the right drive and not erasing data you want to keep. For more information, see "Disk Utility" on page 178.

Usually Disk Utility won't let you erase your startup drive; if you try, you'll get an error. But since you booted from the Snow Leopard Install disk, your usual startup drive isn't busy and Disk Utility will happily erase that drive if you tell it to. To erase a drive, select it from the list on the left side of Disk Utility, click the Erase tab and click Erase. You'll get a warning, and when you choose Erase (instead of Cancel), Disk Utility will go about the business of freeing your hard drive of all that precious data you have built up over the years. A somewhat typical example is shown in Figure 2-2.

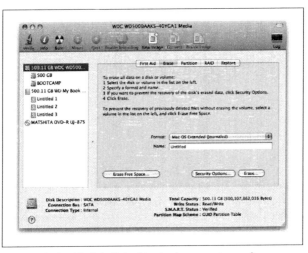

Figure 2-2. An iMac's built-in drive is about to get erased

Once Disk Utility is done erasing your disk, you'll have a blank
drive waiting for a fresh installation of Snow Leopard.

A lot of geeks swore by the Archive and Install method. With
Archive and Install, the installer would copy your System folder
to a folder called Previous System folder. The idea was that Mac
OS X would leave your old settings around in case you needed
them.

The process provided both peace of mind and a certain amount
of geeky certitude for users. Peace of mind is worth a lot, and
you can get it back with a Snow Leopard installation. The most
obvious way to pull off an Archive and Install is to back up
your entire drive (such as with Time Machine or a cloning utility such as Super Duper! or Carbon Copy Cloner) to an external
drive, then do an upgrade on your target drive.

Backing up your entire drive is a great idea, and it is an especially great idea when you are upgrading to a new version of
system software. To be super-safe, back up your entire drive to
an external disk. If you have problems later, you can get any

files you need from the backup or, in a worst case scenario, boot from the copy of your old drive.

A quick and dirty way to duplicate the functionality of Archive and Install is to make copies of key configuration folders such as the System folder. For this, all you need is a little hard drive space, the Finder, and administrative access to your computer: select the System folder, and then choose File→Duplicate from the Finder, and you've got a local copy of it (you'll probably be prompted for your password or the username and password of an administrative user).

If you duplicate the System folder (see Figure 2-3) before you install Snow Leopard, it will be there after you install Snow Leopard. If you have any problems (not likely), you'll be able to crawl through your old System folder to find the solution.

Figure 2-3. A duplicate System folder is much the same as Archive and Install

Beginning the Installation

This is the point where you may, if you wish, customize the installation. Customizing the installation of Snow Leopard isn't necessary, but it does provide the chance to avoid installing things you might never use (certain printer drivers, language translations) and add things that aren't installed by default, like Rosetta (which is needed for applications that run only on PowerPC-based Macs).

If you're not interested in customizing the installation of Snow Leopard, you can skip the next section.

Customizing Snow Leopard's Installation

The default installation of Snow Leopard, whether you're installing Mac OS X on a blank drive or upgrading a Mac running an older version of Mac OS X, is designed to make everybody happy. However, you may not be everybody, and you may have slightly different needs than every other Apple user. If you don't want everything Snow Leopard brings to the table, you can save some disk space (and installation time) by customizing Snow Leopard's installation.

When you click the Customize button, you are presented with a list of things that are about to be installed or skipped. You're probably familiar with checkboxes, but these are a little different from most of the checkboxes you see in Mac OS X. In the installer, you still see the usually checked or unchecked box, but Apple adds a third type of box, one with a line through it to indicate that only some of its options are going to installed (you can expand those options to see what's checked or unchecked under them). Your install options are as follows:

Essential System Software
> You'll see a checkbox, but there is nothing you can actually change. If you want Snow Leopard, you will be installing the essential software.

Printer Support
> This is where you can decide how much hard disk space you want printers to take up. You have four options: None (simply uncheck the box); Printers Used by This Mac, which will require a variable amount of disk space; Nearby

and Popular Printers, which bumps the install 1.4 GB on my machine; and All Available Printers, which increases the amount of required space (over what you'd get if you installed no printers) by roughly 2.7 GB. If you've got plenty of disk space, the All Available Printers is the most flexible option.

Note that Snow Leopard handles printers a little differently from previous versions of OS X. If you choose the Nearby and Popular Printers options, you won't be stuck if you later try to use a printer that isn't installed. Snow Leopard will check with Apple's Software Update to see if a driver exists for the printer you want to use. If it does, it will download and install the driver.

Additional Fonts

Additional fonts is checked by default and the installation is relatively small at 99.2 MB. But if you don't want the fonts, you can uncheck the box and save the space.

Language Translations

Clicking on the triangle reveals a long list of languages you can choose not to have installed. The total package is 1.64 GB, and removing languages you won't use shaves that number down by the amount indicated next each language. Skip them all (English is always installed) and save the full 1.64 GB.

X11

X11 is essential if you're planning on running Unix applications that require the X Window System. If you're going "all Mac, all the time," you can save a paltry 104 MB by skipping the install.

Rosetta

Rosetta allows your Intel Mac to run PowerPC programs. If you have some oldish applications kicking around, or you think you might dig up some oldies, then install Rosetta. The install takes up a measly 2 MB of space, so you'll be gaining functionality without giving up a significant bit of drive space. If you forget to install Rosetta, it isn't a big deal. If you try to start up an application that requires

Rosetta, Mac OS X will alert you with an offer to install Rosetta. It is a quick process and you won't need an install disk because Mac OS X will download Rosetta from Apple via Software Update. You won't even have to restart.

Once you've made your choices (if you make a mistake, clicking the Restore Defaults button will let you start the customization process anew), click OK to move on to the next step of installing Snow Leopard.

At this point you'll have two options: Go Back or Install. If you need to make any changes (such as choosing a different disk to install to), click Go Back. Otherwise, click Install and wait while Snow Leopard installs on your selected destination. You'll likely be pleasantly surprised, as the time it takes for Snow Leopard to install has been significantly reduced compared to earlier versions of Mac OS X.

After the Install

After Snow Leopard is done installing, your Mac will restart using the system you just installed to boot. You'll be treated to an animation welcoming you to Snow Leopard. If the Mac has already been configured—that is, if it has an earlier version of Mac OS X installed—you'll be prompted to register (hit ⌘-Q to skip registration if you wish). Additionally, you might get a message that your mail needs to be upgraded to work with the new version of Mail. Other than that, you can get back to using your Mac just like you used it before you installed Snow Leopard.

If you've installed Snow Leopard onto a blank drive or partition, Snow Leopard will need some more information to get you up and running. You'll select your country and keyboard layout. Then you'll be offered the opportunity to transfer data from another Mac. If you chose not to, click Continue. Next, Snow Leopard will attempt to connect to the Internet. Snow Leopard will automatically try to choose a network option, but if you're not happy with Snow Leopard's choice, you'll find a Different Network Setup button in the lower righthand side of

---

the window. Clicking that button will allow you to control how your Mac connects to the network.

Once you're hooked to the network, you'll be asked for your Apple ID. You can skip this step but if you have a MobileMe account, using that as your Apple ID will let your Mac use MobileMe without further configuration on your part. Once the Apple ID has been entered or dismissed, you'll be offered the opportunity to register. The information you type into the form will be used not just to garner you a spot in Apple's database, but also to generate an address card for you in Address Book and to set up your email address for use with Mail.

Snow Leopard will then ask you for some information on how and where you intend to use your Mac. Once the data collection is out of the way, you will be prompted to set up a user account. Snow Leopard will generate a full name and account name for you. If you don't want to use the suggestions, you can type you own names in. You'll also have to enter a password and, if you wish, a hint in case you forget your password.

With the account created, Snow Leopard will give you the chance to snap a picture for the account with a webcam or choose one from your picture library. Once that is done, Snow Leopard will configure your Mac using your MobileMe information (if you're a member). If you're not a MobileMe member, the process is exactly the same except you'll see a screen where you are prompted to consider purchasing or signing up for a free trial of the MobileMe service.

Moving Data and Applications from Another Mac

Not every user will be installing Snow Leopard from a DVD; some folks will have a new Mac with Snow Leopard preinstalled. If you're one of those lucky ones, you won't be interested in how to install Snow Leopard, as the system is already there. But if you're upgrading from an older Mac, you'll certainly be interested in getting that mountain of data from your old Mac on to your new computer. Apple has an app for that; it is called

Migration Assistant, and you can use it to transfer your files, settings, and preferences from your old Mac to your new one.

NOTE

You might not want to migrate your data from an old Mac right away, as playing with a factory-fresh system can be fun, and migrating data isn't a once-in-a-lifetime opportunity. You can play with your new Mac as much as you like and migrate your data later using Migration Assistant (Applications→Utilities→Migration Assistant).

When you run the Migration Assistant, it can migrate the following:

Users

All your user accounts will be moved to your new Mac. Accounts retain the same privileges (or restrictions) that they had before. If you try to move over a user that already exists on your Mac, you'll have the option to change the name or replace the existing user (as long as you are not logged in as that user; if you want to import settings into your account, use System Preferences→Accounts to create a new user, log in as that user, and run Migration Assistant again). See "Accounts" on page 31 for more information.

Applications

All the applications in the Applications folder are transferred. You won't have to reinstall your applications, and most should retain all their settings (including any registration or activation needed to run).

Settings

Have a bunch of saved networks and passwords in your Network Preferences? They all come along for a ride. So, if you're used to automatically jumping on at the local Wi-Fi hot spot, you'll get on without any extra effort. Your screen saver requires a password to get back to the desktop? It still will. There are three suboptions under this one:

Time Zone, Machine (computer settings other than network or time zone), and Network.

Other files and folders

If your Mac has files strewn everywhere, even if they aren't where Mac OS X expects them to be (the Documents directory), they will be transferred.

NOTE

If you stashed any files in the System folder, they won't come along for the ride. But you shouldn't ever stash anything in the System folder, as it can get modified at any time (even by security updates and the like).

Migration Assistant does not move:

The System folder

You're installing a new system, so there isn't a reason for the old System folder to come along for the ride.

Apple applications and utilities

Migration Assistant assumes that every Apple application that came with Snow Leopard on the system you are transferring data to is newer or the same as the corresponding item on the Mac you are transferring data from.

After running Migration Assistant, your new Mac will seem a lot like your old Mac. As you can probably guess, you'll need to be logged in as an administrative user (or be able to supply the username and password of an administrative user) to run Migration Assistant.

If you haven't migrated data since the MacBook Air came out, the process has changed a little bit. In the days before the Air, Migration Assistant worked by utilizing FireWire Target Disk Mode. You'd start the computer you wanted to transfer data from in FireWire Target Disk mode (hold down ⌘-T while booting or choose the Start in Target Disk Mode option from the Startup Disk Preference pane), plug it into the destination Mac, and Migration Assistant would take care of the rest. The good news is that this method still works if you have two computers with FireWire; the better news is that if you don't have two Macs with FireWire, you can still use Migration Assistant. In fact, Migration Assistant offers three ways to get your old data on your new Mac:

From another Mac

Choosing this option allows you to transfer data from a Mac either wired or on the same network (wired or wireless) to your Mac. You can use a Mac connected directly via a FireWire cable, networked via Ethernet, or on the same wireless network as your Mac. Clicking Continue brings up two choices: Use FireWire or Use Network. Choosing FireWire brings up a pane where you can select what you want transferred. You can choose Users, Applications, Settings, and Other files and folders on (disk name).

NOTE

If you don't have FireWire on your Mac, you won't get a choice. Migration Assistant will instead assume you want to use the network.

Things are a little more complicated if you choose Use Network. First, you'll need to write down the number that's shown on the screen. Then head over to the Mac you want to transfer the data from. Open Migration Assistant (make sure you have the latest software updates before you proceed) and choose "To another Mac." You'll get a window showing you the other Mac(s) running Migration Assistant and a place to type in the code.

NOTE

Planning ahead helps at this point; for Migration Assistant to work, all other applications must be closed. Save all your work and quit everything before you open Migration Assistant. Once the computers have made friends, you'll get the option to transfer the data you wish to be transferred.

From a Time Machine backup or other disk

This is the option you'll choose if you want the classic version of Migration Assistant. Connect a drive to your Mac; it can be another Mac started in FireWire Target Disk mode if your Macs both have FireWire, a bootable USB drive, or a drive with a Time Machine backup. Next, select the "From a Time Machine backup or another disk" option and click Continue. You'll be presented with a list of drives you can import data from in the next window. Select the drive you want and click Continue.

To another Mac

This option is here to complete the "From another Mac" option. If you use one, you'll have to use the other.

Fine Tuning Data Migration

If you're migrating data, chances are you have a new Mac. If you're like most users, you've accumulated a lot of cruft over time, and you might not want everything to transfer from your old Mac. Do you really want to save that folder of LOLcat pictures? Well, of course you'll want to save that, but that folder with your masters thesis is just taking up space. Migration Assistant allows you (for Users and Settings) to decide what to take and what to leave behind. Don't worry, this is a nondestructive process; the data you shun on your new Mac will still be on the old Mac.

To decide what you want to leave behind, click on the right facing triangle to expand your options as shown in Figure 2-4.

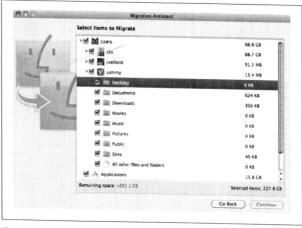

Figure 2-4. Uncheck what you don't want on your new Mac

After your selections are made, click Continue and your data will be transferred. Give it some time and your data will magically appear on your new Mac.

NOTE

Don't get confused by the folder names. For example, Movies doesn't mean that Migration Assistant will import all movies; it means it will import the *Movies* folder. If you have movies stored elsewhere and you want them to come along during the transfer, make sure "All other files and folders" is checked.

Once Migration Assistant has finished migrating your data, Setup Assistant will pop up and offer to upgrade your email (if you're migrating from an older version of Mac OS X). This takes a few moments, but once it is finished, you are free to use your new Mac and pick up where you left off with the old one!

CHAPTER 3

The Quick Guide to Snow Leopard

What You Need To Know About Mac OS X

Finding your way around Snow Leopard for the first time is exciting, but it is also easy to miss out on many cool new features, especially if you are new to Mac OS X or if you've been using an older version of the operating system. This chapter will get you up to speed on the basics of Mac OS X, with a special focus on what's new in Snow Leopard. Topics covered include accounts, your Home folder, logging in and out of your Mac, and much more. The goal of this chapter is to familiarize you with the most important aspects of using Mac OS X so you can get the most out of Apple's best operating system to date. The logical place to start is with the first thing you created when you installed or ran Mac OS X for the first time—your account.

Accounts

Snow Leopard is the latest and greatest from Apple but the roots of the operating system go very far back, to the Unix operating system. Unix is a multiuser workstation and server operating system; because Mac OS X is based on Unix, it is also multiuser to its core. Even if no one but you ever touches your

Mac, it is still helpful to understand user accounts, because you may need to deal with them someday. Consider these possible reasons:

- As you will learn shortly, you may want to set up an unprivileged account for day-to-day use to limit your vulnerability to mistakes and malicious software.

- If you ever need to run a demonstration on your Mac, you probably will want to create a separate user to run the demo and completely avoid the possibility of interruptions from chat buddies, calendar reminders, and the like.

- Even the most solitary Mac user eventually needs to let someone else (a houseguest, family member, or customs agent) use their Mac, and it is so easy to set up a new user that you may as well do it—then even your most reckless friend can use your Mac without much threat of major chaos.

There are five types of user accounts in Mac OS X, and you can also create groups of users (creating accounts is discussed in "Setting up accounts" on page 34):

Administrator

When you create your first account in Mac OS X, it will be an Administrator account. This is the most powerful account because an administrator can make *global* changes that affect the computer and all other user accounts. (For example, an administrator can add and remove programs for everyone.) Because of this ability to change things (sometimes inadvertently) for everyone with an account on your Mac, most savvy Mac users argue that an Administrator account should not be used for day-to-day computing; instead, a Standard account should be used most of the time.

Standard

Standard accounts are the sweet spot. You're not going to mess up your Mac or anyone else's account using a Standard account, but you still have plenty of control over how your Mac works while you are using your machine. You can add and delete programs to your account but not to the entire system. You can delete files you own but not files owned by others. If you find a lot of the fun of owning a computer is messing it up, and then going back and fixing the mess, the good news is that you can still mess up your own account.

Managed with Parental Controls

Accounts managed with Parental Controls are limited in what they can do. Users won't be able to make changes to the system at all. If you tried to use a managed account, you'd likely find it frustrating and unacceptable. To a five-year-old, the managed account is nirvana. You can adjust the settings with the Parental Controls preference pane.

Sharing Only

Sharing Only accounts are set up for people to connect from another computer to share files. People assigned this type of account can't log in to your Mac via the log in window; only remote connections are accepted.

Guest

This account is fantastic if you want to let someone use your Mac without being able to make any permanent changes. Log someone in as a Guest and they'll be able to search the Web, check their email on the Web, and much more. The moment they log out, everything they did, any data they downloaded, and so on is gone. You can even enable parental controls for a guest account if you are worried about guests doing things you'd rather they did not do.

Group

You can use Group accounts to create a group that multiple users are a member of. This can be used to exercise fine-grained control over privileges for shared documents.

Setting up accounts

Once you know the differences between accounts in Snow Leopard, you'll likely want to set up a few or a few dozen accounts. Click the Apple menu and choose System Preferences, and then click Accounts (located in the System section). This loads the Accounts preference pane. Before you can make any changes, you have to click the lock icon at the bottom of the preference pane, and enter an administrator username and password. The extra level of security is there because when you're using the Accounts preference pane, you have the ability to adjust the level of access for other accounts. You wouldn't want someone making a change here while your computer is unattended.

To add a new account, press the + button directly above the lock icon. Clicking the + button opens a drop-down window where you'll be able to select the type of account to create, type in the identifying information (full name, account name), and set up a password. If you want to take a picture for the new account, after the account is created click on the account picture and choose Edit Picture. You will get the option of choosing a new picture from a file or taking one with your Mac's built-in iSight or attached webcam.

To enable the Guest account, click it in the list of accounts, and check the box marked "Allow guests to log in to this computer." This will add a guest entry to the login window. Guests won't need a password to use your Mac.

The Home Folder

The Home folder is what makes your Mac seem like your Mac. If you create a document and save it in Documents, the document doesn't show up in some centralized documents folder for the entire system (like the Applications folder), it shows up in the folder called Documents inside your Home folder.

This pattern extends into other folders (Music, Movies, Pictures, and more). Each account you create gets its own Home folder with a subset of folders. To take a look at all the Home folders on your Mac, open the Finder and navigate to your system drive (the drive you boot your Mac from). Open the *Users* directory to see the Home folder of all the accounts on your Mac. The Home folder for the current user will look like a little house; this is where all your files and personal preferences (your selected desktop background, for example) are stored.

NOTE

There's one folder in Users—Shared—that doesn't correspond to any user. You can use this folder to store files and folders you need to share between users on the same Mac.

You can access your Home folder quickly by opening a Finder window and clicking on the house icon in the sidebar (or choosing Go from the menu and choosing Home). In every Home folder you'll find the following list of standard subfolders:

Documents
> This is the default location for saving documents. Using the Documents folder is not mandatory, but it does offer a level of convenience to have a central repository for all your documents. You can add subfolders to the Documents folder for even more organization. Just open the

Documents folder and choose New Folder from the Finders's File menu (Shift-⌘-N).

Desktop

This is where all the files sitting on the desktop are stored. There are a few items (hard disks, CDs, DVDs, iPods, and servers) that can appear on the desktop, but you won't see when you're looking in this folder. If you drag a document from this folder to the Trash, it will disappear from the desktop.

Downloads

The Downloads folder serves double duty: it is a folder in your Home directory but it also has a spot on your Dock. Anything you download from the Web via a browser shows up here (unless you change the default download location in your browser's preferences) and shows up on your Dock in the Download stack (the Download stack bounces when a new item finishes downloading). If you click the Save button next to an attachment in Mail, it also is saved here. You can get your downloaded items either from the Downloads folder or from the downloads stack on the Dock.

Library

You usually won't interact with this folder (unless something goes wrong, in which case, see "Misbehaving Applications" on page 100), but the programs you use make changes to this folder all the time. Mac OS X stores your configuration files, caches, and even some data (such as iCal calendars) here. For example, if you poke around in the *Library/Preferences* folder, you'll see it full of *.plist* (property list) files, which contain configuration information for Mac OS X applications.

Movies

This is another folder in your Home directory for your convenience. It is much like the Documents folder, only Apple has put it there for you to store all the movies you make with iMovie and the screencasts you make with QuickTime Player. As with the *Documents* folder, there's no reason other than convenience for you to store your movies here.

Music

The Music folder is where you can store music files. It is also where iTunes stores its music library and online purchases, including iPhone/iPod applications and videos.

Pictures

What could the Pictures folder be for? Perhaps pictures. Toss all your *.jpg*, *.png*, *.gif* files right in here. iPhoto also uses the Pictures folder to store the pictures you add to iPhoto.

Public

The Public folder exists as a repository for files you want to share with other users who can log in to your Mac. They can get to it by using the Finder to navigate to */Users/User name/Public*. If you want to share files from your Public folder with people using other computers, you'll have to go to the Sharing Preference pane (see "Sharing" on page 142).

NOTE

The / in front of *Users* indicates that you should open your computer's startup drive in the Finder, then look for the *Users* directory and drill down from there.

To receive files from others, use the *Drop Box*. The Drop Box is a folder that resides in the Public folder as a place for users to put files for you. Drop Box is a shared folder (if you open it, you'll note that is has a gray band across the top that says Shared Folder) but sharing only goes one way. People can put things into your Drop Box, but they can't take anything out. In fact, they can't even see the contents of the folder.

Sites

If you want your Mac to host a website (it is certainly capable), this is where you put the files for it. You'll need to do more than add an HTML file to the Sites folder to get it working, though. See "Sharing" on page 142 to start sharing sites stored in the Sites folder over your local network.

Using Snow Leopard

Once you have Snow Leopard running, and have your system set up, what do you need to know to use it? That is what this section is all about. You'll learn the basics you need to know to start up your Mac, get around after you've booted, and shut the machine down.

Starting Up

Chapter 2 covered what happens when you turn on a fresh, out-of-the-box Mac (or a new install of Snow Leopard). Each time you boot up your Mac after that, the startup experience is usually seamless.

By default, your Mac has only one operating system, Mac OS X. When you start your Mac, it will boot into Mac OS X. Your Mac doesn't have to be a one-system machine, though; with a little effort, you can run multiple operating systems. However, this section deals with a Mac OS X-based start sequence.

NOTE

If you've installed Boot Camp or another operating system, you can set the default startup disk with the Startup Disk Preference pane (System Preferences→Startup Disk).

The first thing you'll see when you start your Mac is the grey Apple logo, followed by the spinning wheel that resembles a circle of perpetually falling dominoes. Once your Mac has finished booting, you'll be logged in. If you don't have automatic login enabled, you'll be presented with a list of users or a username/password prompt, depending on your settings (see "Logging In" on page 40 for more details). Log in with your username and password, and you'll be transported to the Mac OS X desktop.

Startup key commands

Before your Mac starts booting up, you can press one of these key combinations to change how it starts:

Key command	Action
Hold mouse button while powering on	Ejects any media in the optical drive
C	Forces your Mac to start up from a CD or DVD in the optical drive
R	Resets display for Macs with built-in displays (MacBooks and iMacs) back to the original (factory) settings
T	Boots the Mac in FireWire Target Disk Mode if the Mac has a FireWire port; to get out of FireWire Target Disk Mode restart the Mac
⌘-S	Boots in Single User Mode, which starts your Mac with a text-only console where you can perform some expert-level system maintenance; see "AppleJack" on page 112 for some tips on using Single User Mode
⌘-V	Boots in verbose mode, which shows all the kernel and startup messages while your Mac is booting
Shift	Boots into Safe mode, a reduced functionality mode that forces a check of your startup disk, loads only the most important kernel extensions, disables fonts not in the /System/Library/Fonts folder, and more
Option	Invokes Startup Manager and allows you to select which OS to boot into; useful if you have multiple copies of Mac OS X installed or use Boot Camp to run other operating systems

Logging In

By default, your Mac is set up to log in as the user you created when you first set it up (Automatic Login). This is something of a security risk, since anyone can get into your account simply by powering up your Mac. If you have multiple people using your Mac, you will likely want to turn this option off. Click the Apple menu, choose System Preferences, and go to the Accounts Preference pane. Click the lock at the bottom left to unlock the options on this pane. Next, click Login Options and set Automatic Login to off.

You can also turn on Fast User Switching with Login Options. This lets you switch users without having to log off, so the applications that you have running keep going while another user logs into their account. Having more than one user logged in can use up quite a bit of memory, so if you have less than 2 GB of RAM, you might want to use this sparingly.

If you have Fast User Switching enabled, look for an icon or username menu on the right side of the menu bar. Click this menu and use the drop-down menu to select another user to log in as. If you don't enable Fast User Switching, you'll have to log out (Apple Menu→Log Out) before you can log in as a different user.

Logging Out, Sleeping, and Shutting Down

Using the Mac is great, but at some point you'll want to stop using it. When you're ready to stop, you've got options:

Shut Down

    To shut down your Mac, click the Apple menu and choose Shut Down. Click Shut Down in the dialogue that appears, and your Mac will power off. It should only take a few seconds. The next time you want to use your Mac, hit the power button and wait for the machine to boot.

Log Out

To close your current work session, but leave your Mac running, you can just log out by clicking the Apple menu and choosing Log Out (or by pressing Shift-⌘-Q). Click Log Out in the dialogue box that appears. Shift-Option-⌘-Q logs you out immediately. This quits all your running programs. To use the Mac again, you (or another user) will need to log in.

Sleep

You don't have to shut your Mac down every day; you can just let it sleep. On a MacBook all you have to do is close the lid. On desktop Macs (or MacBooks), select Sleep from the Apple menu or press Option-⌘-Eject. A sleeping Mac uses very little electricity, and your Mac will wake from sleep in seconds. (For information on saving energy, see "Energy Saver" on page 130.)

Shut down and log out key commands

No one wants to spend unnecessary amounts of time logging out or shutting down. Following are the key commands to make the process faster:

Key command	Action
Shift-⌘-Q	Logs out
Shift-Option-⌘-Q	Logs out without warning dialogue
Apple Menu→Shut Down	Shuts your Mac down; hold Option when selecting (or type Control-Option-⌘-Eject) to shut down immediately
Apple Menu→Restart	Restarts your Mac; hold Option when selecting (or type Control-⌘-Eject) to restart immediately
Control-Eject	Activates a window containing options to Restart, Shut Down, Sleep, or Cancel
Control-⌘-Power Button	Forces shutdown of your Mac (use this only as a last resort)
Option-⌘-Eject	Puts your Mac to sleep

Snow Leopard Basics

There's a lot that happens between start up and shut down on
your Mac—that is the time you are using your computer to get
things done (or have fun). Your time spent in Mac OS X will
be more pleasant and productive if you learn where everything
is. The logical place to start the tour is right at the top of your
screen, with the ubiquitous menu bar.

The Menu Bar

The menu bar spans the top of your monitor (if you use multiple monitors, you can choose which monitor the menu bar
shows up on with the Displays Preference pane) and provides
access to commonly used commands on the left side while the
right side is reserved for *menu extras* (called menulets by some
users) and Spotlight (the magnifying glass icon). Every Mac
user's menu bar is likely to look a little different, depending on
what's installed and how the Mac is configured. A fairly typical
menu bar is shown in Figure 3-1.

Figure 3-1. A typical menu bar

Here's what you'll find in the menu bar:

1. The Apple menu
2. The Application menu
3. A typical set of application menus
4. Menu extras
5. Spotlight

The first entry you'll see in the menu bar if you move from left to right is the Apple menu. No matter which application you're using, the options found when clicking the Apple menu will be the same (see Figure 3-2).

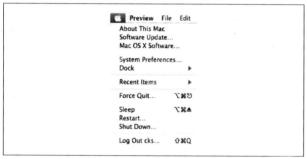

Figure 3-2. Snow Leopard's Apple menu

Here's a description of all the Apple menu entries:

About this Mac

Pops up a window giving you a quick overview of your Mac: version number of Mac OS X, the processor, and the amount of RAM you have installed.

There are three things you can click on in the About This Mac window:

- Click the version number (such as 10.6) to cycle through the build number of Mac OS X and the serial number of your Mac. It's not unusual to need this information when getting support over the phone.

- Click Software Update to see whether you have all the latest and greatest updates installed.

- Click the More Info button to open System Profiler, which reveals scads of information about your Mac. You will be able to access information about the hardware, your network, and any software installed on your Mac.

Software Update...

Launches the Software Update application. This only checks for Apple-supplied software, and doesn't check for updates to any third-party software.

Mac OS X Software

Takes you to *http://www.apple.com/downloads* where you can get a look at the latest software from Apple and others.

System Preferences

Launches the System Preferences application. For more on System Preferences, see Chapter 5.

Dock

Opens a menu to let you quickly configure some Dock options: Turn Hiding On, Turn Magnification On, and three choices of where you want the Dock positioned (anywhere but the top). The Dock... option opens the Dock Preference pane.

Recent Items

Displays a menu showing your 10 most recently used applications, 10 most recently opened documents, and 10 most recently used servers. You can change the number of items displayed by going to System Preferences→Appearance and adjusting the "Number of recent items" settings.

Force Quit...

Lets you force stubborn applications to quit. For more information, see Chapter 5.

Sleep

Puts your Mac to sleep. Sleep is a low-power mode that preserves what you were doing before the Mac went to sleep. When you wake your Mac from sleep, everything will be just as you left it. Waking your Mac from sleep is simple; just press a key or move the mouse and your Mac will wake up in seconds.

You can set your Mac to automatically sleep after a period of inactivity of your choice by using the Energy Saver Preference pane (see "Energy Saver" on page 130).

Restart

Restarts your Mac. Your Mac will shut down and immediately reboot, and you'll go through the entire startup process. You'll be asked to confirm that you really want to restart your Mac. If you don't hit Cancel, your Mac will restart one minute after selecting this menu option.

Shut Down...

Powers your Mac down. It will stay shut down until you press the power button, unless you've set a time for you Mac to auto start in the Energy Saver Preference pane (see "Energy Saver" on page 130).

Log Out...

Logs you out of your user account. The next time someone uses your Mac, they will have to log in.

NOTE

In the Apple menu, you'll notice many of the options have three periods after them. The periods indicate that a confirmation dialogue will appear. If you want to Restart, Shut Down, or Log Out without seeing the dialogue, hold the Option key while selecting the action of your choice from the Apple menu.

The Application menu

Next to the Apple menu is the Application menu. The exact contents of the Application menu depends on what application is currently being used (the leftmost Application menu will have the name of the application in bold letters). Figure 3-3 shows the Finder's Application menu.

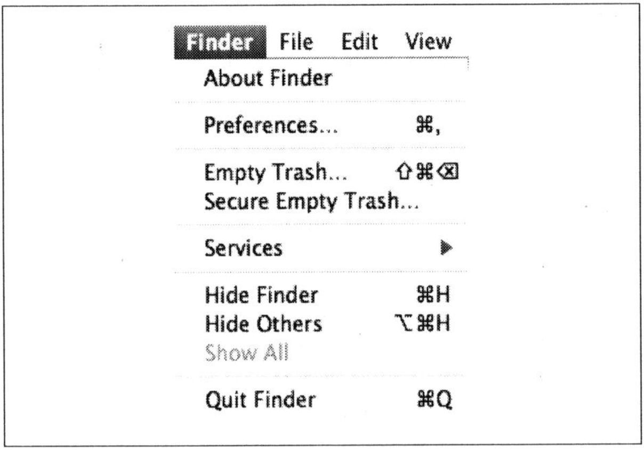

Figure 3-3. The Finder's Application menu

There really isn't a standard Application menu but there are some commonalities in most. In the typical Application menu you'll find:

About Application Name

Opens a window with the version number of the application, copyright information, and whatever else the developer of an application thinks should be there.

Preferences...

Opens the application's preferences. What you can control using the Preferences... option varies from application to application and can be very little or a great deal. For information on the Finder's preference, see "Mastering the Finder" on page 54.

Services

Services has changed a good deal since Leopard. In Leopard, the Services menu brought up a few options to hand off tasks to other application. Now Services is much more customizable. See "The Services Menu" on page 48 for more details.

Hide ApplicationName

Hides all of the application's windows. If you have 50 Safari windows open and don't want to minimize each one to see what lies beneath, choose this option. To get the windows back, just click on the application's icon in the Dock.

Hide Others

Hides every application except the application you are using.

Show All

The antidote to the Hide command. If you've hidden a single application or every application, Show All will return all the hidden application windows to full visibility.

Quit Application Name

Quits the current application. You can also invoke it with ⌘-Q. Most people's inclination is to quit any application they aren't using, but that often isn't necessary. Mac OS X is very good at resource allocation, so leaving an application idling will generally have very little impact on the system.

The Services Menu

The Services menu has been redone for Snow Leopard and is the most complex option found in the Application menu. It offers you quick access to functions provided by other programs. The services available to you depend on the applications installed on your Mac and the program you are using. TextEdit (available in the *Applications* folder) provides a nice example of what the Services menu can do for you. Figure 3-4 shows the options available when you've selected some text in Text Edit. If you want to send the selected text as a Mail message, all you need do is choose Send Selection and Mail will pop open a new message with the text already inserted.

In some applications the Services menu will have nothing to offer (the menu will read "No Services Apply"). Clicking the Services Preferences option opens the Keyboard Preference pane to its Services section, where you can customize the Services menu. You can create your own services with Automator.

Standard Application menus

After the Application menu comes more menus. How many? That depends on the application. Mail has eight and Safari has seven. The number of menus is dependent on the application and how clever the developers were. The variability noted, without exception, you'll find at least four menus besides the Application menu in the menu bar. What is actually in those four menus also varies depending on the application, but there are some standard options to expect:

File

> Typically this menu will contain options for saving, opening, creating, and printing files.

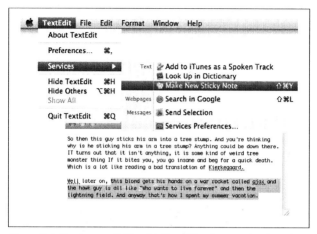

Figure 3-4. Services available with TextEdit when text is selected

Edit

Here you will find the old Mac standbys: Cut (⌘-X), Copy (⌘-C), Paste (⌘-V) and Undo (⌘-Z).

Window

This menu will list all the open windows for a particular application.

Help

Depending on the application, the Help window can either be very useful or a waste of space. Whether the help is going to be worthwhile or not is completely dependent on the developer, but it is invoked in the same way. Click the Help menu or press Shift-⌘-?.

When you open the Help menu, you'll see a search box and more options. One of the really nice things about the Help menu in Mac OS X is that it won't just regurgitate an entry in a database to read. If possible, Help will show you how to do what you want to do. Suppose you want to create a new folder while using the Finder. Open the Finder's Help menu, type **new folder** in the Help search box, and hover your mouse over the New Folder entry that appears. The Help system will show you which menu has the New Folder option and highlight it with a floating blue arrow as shown in Figure 3-5.

Figure 3-5. Help can find the menu item you need

Menu extras

On the right side of the menu bar is where you'll find the menu extras (Spotlight is on the far right and isn't technically a menu extra). Menu extras allow easy access to an often used function. The menu extra's icon usually reflects what it actually does. A useful example is the Keychain menu extra (Figure 3-6). You can add this extra by going to the Keychain Access utility in */Applications/Utilities* and choosing "Show Status in Menu Bar" from its preferences. It gives you quick access to your passwords and secure notes without having to make a trip to the Utilities folder.

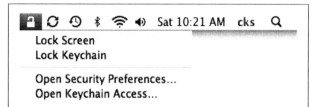

Figure 3-6. The Keychain menu extra

Not every menu extra is a shortcut to a program; some menu extras control settings (such as the Volume menu extra) and some are there to show the status of certain aspects of your Mac (such as the Battery menu extra). What menu extras you find useful depends on how you use your Mac.

Even with the wide variety of things menu extras can do, there are a few things about menu extras that don't change. It doesn't matter if you're using Safari or iTunes, the menu extras you have in your menu bar will stay the same and their functionality will remain unchanged.

If you just can't get enough of menu extras (what menu extras show up by default on your Mac depend on how your Mac is configured), you can look in */System/Library/CoreServices/ Menu Extras* to see all the menu extras included with Snow Leopard (menu extras are appended with .menu). Double-click any of the 25 items found in that folder to put the menu extra in your menu bar. Note that some Menu Bar items won't show up on some Macs. For example, if you try to add a Battery menu extra to the Menu Bar of an iMac, your efforts will be for naught, since it has no battery. This is also the place to go if you can't figure out how to restore a menu extra you've removed.

You can banish unwanted menu extras by ⌘-clicking them (hold ⌘ while clicking) and dragging the unwanted menu extra off the menu bar. The menu extra will disappear with a satisfying poof sound and an accompanying animation. If you want to reorder your menu extras, ⌘-click and drag to arrange them in any order you want. Note that you can't move the Spotlight icon. While Spotlight might look like a menu extra, as far as Mac OS X is concerned, it is immovable and permanent.

The Accounts menu

If you've enabled Fast User Switching, you'll see the account name of the currently logged-on user here or a small icon. Click it to select another user to log in as.

Spotlight

This brings up the Spotlight Search menu. For more information, see "Searching with Spotlight" on page 88.

Use the menu bar less

Following is a quick list of some of the most commonly used keyboard shortcuts for items on the menu bar. Note that specific applications have their own keyboard commands that can streamline your workflow, so investigating the keyboard commands for the applications you use frequently is worth your time.

Key command	Action
⌘-C	Copies selected information to the clipboard
⌘-V	Pastes the contents of the clipboard
⌘-X	Cuts the selection and copies it to the clipboard
⌘-A	Selects everything (the entire document, all items in a folder, etc.)
⌘-S	Saves the current file (you can't use this one too much)
⌘-O	Opens new file
⌘-W	Closes the current window
⌘-Z	Undoes most recent action (some programs offer multiple levels of undo)
⌘-H	Hides the current application and its windows
⌘-,	Opens the current application's Preferences
⌘-Q	Quits the program (not available in Finder)

There are many more key commands at your disposal (see Chapter 9), but the commands listed are likely to be the ones you use most often.

The Desktop

Continuing the tour of your Mac, the big area under the menu bar is the desktop. Open application windows float over the desktop. Depending on how you have it configured, the desktop will also show you all the attached and internal drives (iPods, flash drives, and so on), any optical disks (CDs, DVDs), and any files you've stored on the desktop for easy access. You can change your desktop background by either Control-clicking or right-clicking the desktop and choosing Change Desktop Background or by heading to the Desktop & Screen Saver Preference pane (see Chapter 5).

To control how items are displayed on the desktop, either Control-click or right-click a blank area of the desktop and choose Show View Options. You can also choose Show View Options from the Finder's View menu (⌘-J), as shown in Figure 3-7.

Figure 3-7. The View Options menu

With the View Options menu you'll be able to control the icon size (between 16×16 pixels all the way to 128×128), the grid spacing (there is an invisible grid that Mac OS X uses when cleaning up the desktop), the text size of the labels of items on the desktop, and the positioning of the labels.

If you opt to check the Show Item Info box, you'll get extra information when looking at items on your desktop. Drives will show the name of the drive and the amount of free space left, folders will list the name of the folder and the number of items the folder contains, and DVDs will show the size of the data. The extra information displayed with files depends on the file type. Images, for example, display the size of the images in pixels. Show icon preview switches between generic icons and icons that display the file's contents.

Finally, you'll be able to choose how you want the desktop to arrange the items. You can choose to have the items snap to the grid or be arranged according to some criteria (name, date created, and so on).

To navigate on the desktop without using the mouse, you can use the arrow keys (they work as you would expect) or you can start typing the item's name. The item you are looking for will automatically be highlighted and you can open it by hitting the ⌘-O key while the item is highlighted. Hitting the Return key allows you to rename the item.

To control what kind of items are shown on the desktop, you'll have to use the Finder's Preferences (switch to the Finder and hit ⌘-, or open the Preferences menu under the Finder's Application menu). Under the General tab, you'll find options to display (or not display) Hard Disks, External Disks, CDs, DVDs, and iPods, and Connected Servers.

Mastering the Finder

Click some empty space on the desktop to bring the Finder to the front (you can also click its Dock icon, or hit ⌘-Tab until you select its icon). When you're using Snow Leopard, you'll be using the Finder quite often. The Finder is used to move files, copy files, and launch applications, among other things.

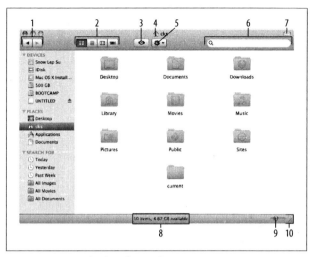

Figure 3-8. A standard Finder window

Understanding the Finder is key to successfully getting around in Mac OS X. The most common way users interact with the Finder is through a Finder window, discussed next.

The Finder window

Figure 3-8 shows a typical Finder window.

The Finder window is made up of several components:

1. Back and forward buttons

These buttons cycle you through directories you've been using. A typical example would be starting in your Home directory and drilling down into your Documents folder. After you've found the document you were looking for, clicking the back button returns you to your Home directory.

2. View controls

These four buttons control how the Finder's information is displayed. You have four options: Icon View (default),

List View, Column View, and Cover Flow. These are discussed in "Finder views" on page 61.

3. *Quick look*

Quick Look offers a preview of the selected item (see Quickly look inside a file on page 65 for more information).

4. *Proxy icon*

The tiny graphical representation of the current folder next to the title is called the Proxy icon. You can drag the Proxy icon to move the folder or hold Option-drag to create a copy.

5. *Action menu*

Clicking this reveals a drop-down menu that varies depending on the item selected. Generally, the list contains the same options as if you right-clicked or Control-clicked an item.

6. *Search*

Entering text in this box and hitting Return tells the Finder to search for items matching your criteria. The search is powered by Spotlight, but unlike a Spotlight Search, it won't return Mail messages or web pages.

7. *Hide/show toolbar and sidebar*

The oblong button allows you to hide the toolbar and the sidebar. If you've already banished the sidebar and toolbar, clicking this button reveals them.

8. *Summary*

This reveals the number of items in the current folder and the space remaining on your disk.

9. *Size slider*

This option only shows up in Icon View and allows you to adjust the size of the icons.

10. *Resize window control*

Grab this handle and you can resize the window to fit your viewing needs.

Customizing the Finder toolbar

To remove items from the Finder's toolbar hold the ⌘ key, click on the item you want gone, and drag it off of the toolbar. Removing items from the toolbar might tidy things up a bit but it doesn't give you what most people want: *more* options. To get more options, you want to add things to your toolbar, not take them away. You can do that with Snow Leopard. You can either right-click or Control-click on a blank space in the toolbar or go to View→Customize Toolbar. A new dialogue box will open showing all the items you can add, as shown in Figure 3-9.

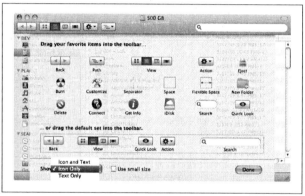

Figure 3-9. That's a lot of options!

Clicking Show allows you to change how items in the Finder's toolbar are displayed, rather what is displayed. You get three options: Icon only (default), Icon and Text, and Text only. Most of the items you can add are self-explanatory, but a few are worthy of a deeper look.

Path

    Adding a Path button to your toolbar gives you a menu that shows the path up from the current directory to the top-level of your computer. For example, suppose you have the Finder open to your *Pictures* folder. Clicking the Path button will reveal options for:

- Pictures
- Your Home folder
- Users
- Your Boot Drive
- Computer

You can choose any location in the list to go immediately to that directory.

Burn

Burn a lot of disks? Select the item (or folder), click the Burn button, and the Finder will tell you to insert a disk to burn to.

Get Info

This brings up the Info window for any selected item. Very useful if you adjust permissions often.

The sidebar

The sidebar occupies the lefthand side of a Finder window and is reminiscent of iTunes' sidebar. The Finder divides the sidebar into four sections:

DEVICES

This is where you will find the devices connected to your Mac, including internal drives, your iDisk (if you have one), external drives, USB sticks, iPods, CDs, and DVDs.

SHARED

Will list any shared devices available to your Mac. Computers shared via Bonjour, shared drives, Time Capsule, Back to My Mac, and the like will show up here.

PLACES

A grouping of popular destinations on your Mac. If you find the default list (Desktop, your Home folder, Applications, and Documents) not inclusive enough for your tastes, you can drag folders or files to the PLACES section of the sidebar.

SEARCH FOR

Contains predefined searches Apple thinks you'll find relevant to your day-to-day computing needs. By default, you get searches for items that have been added or changed for the past day, yesterday, and past week. You also get three Smart folders that will reveal all the images, movies, and documents on your Mac. These Smart folders aren't shortcuts to any particular folder; they contain all the items anywhere on your Mac that meet the criteria specified by the Smart folder (see "Smart Folders" on page 83).

The sidebar provides more functionality than merely a speedy way to open up these locations. The Eject icon next to Drives can be used to eject them. Want to install an application you just downloaded? Instead of opening a Finder window to the Applications folder, just drag the application to the Application folder in the sidebar. Reordering the sidebar is a simple matter of dragging the items to your preferred order, and removing items from the sidebar is as easy as dragging them off of the sidebar. Dragging an item out the sidebar won't delete the item, it only deletes the reference to the folder from the sidebar. Finally, there's a new feature in Snow Leopard: you can remove categories from the sidebar. See the next section for more details.

Finder preferences

Like every application, the Finder has a set of preferences you can customize. To access the preferences you can either go to the Finder Applications menu and choose Preferences, or type ⌘-, while the Finder is the active application. Once there, you get a lot of control over just what the Finder shows you and where it shows up.

The Finder's Preference window has four buttons. You get to control:

General

Here you determine what items show up on the desktop. By checking a box, you have Hard Disks, External Disks, CDs, DVDs, iPods and Connected Servers show up on the desktop. You can also specify what a new Finder window opens. The default is your Home folder but you can change that to any folder with a pop-up menu under "New Finder windows open:". You also get a checkbox (unchecked by default) where you can choose to open folders in a new window. Finally you can fine tune (or turn off) *spring-loaded* folders. Spring-loaded folders automatically pop open if you drag an item over them, allowing you to quickly access nested folders while dragging an item.

Labels

If you are big into organization, you can label items with a color code. The default is to have the colors match the label name. For example, if you label something with the color red, the text label is red. That isn't very descriptive, so if you want to have the text label of *En Fuego*, instead of just red, you can change the label name. Note that changing the label won't impact how the labeled folder is displayed.

Sidebar

This button allows you to specify which items are displayed in the sidebar. Check to show; uncheck to hide. If you've dragged a built-in item out of the sidebar a trip to this section of the Finder's preferences can restore it. If you uncheck all the items under a category, the category will no longer appear in the sidebar. (If you've added any items to that section of the sidebar, the category won't vanish until you also remove the items by dragging them out of the sidebar.)

Advanced

The Advanced button gives you checkboxes to control if filename extensions are revealed (if the box is checked, Safari will be displayed as Safari.app), if the Finder should warn you before changing an extension, if you should be

---

warned before emptying the Trash, and if the Trash should be emptied securely (for more on Trash, see "The Dock" on page 69).

Finder views

The Finder has four views you can choose from: Icon View (default), List View, Column View, and Cover Flow. You can change them using the toolbar buttons described in "Customizing the Finder toolbar" on page 57.

Icon View (⌘-1)

Icon View is the default view in Snow Leopard. Items are displayed as either a file icon, an application icon, or a folder icon as shown in Figure 3-10.

Single-clicking an item in Icon view selects it; double-clicking launches an application, opens a file (inside the associated application), or opens a folder.

You can use the keyboard arrows to move from item to item. Holding the Shift key while using the keyboard arrows selects multiple items.

Figure 3-10. Icon view of the Applications folder

List View (⌘-2)

List View presents the contents of a folder as a list. You can follow subfolders by clicking the disclosure triangles. See Figure 3-11.

List View offers more information than Icon View, but has a more cluttered feel. As with Icon View, you can navigate through List View by using the arrow keys on your keyboard. Up and down changes the selection. Right and left opens and closes a subfolder's disclosure arrow. To open all subfolders under the one you're opening, use Option-right arrow; to close all subfolders after you've opened them, use Option-left arrow. If you want to sort the files, click on the row headings. The arrow in the row heading indicates the order of the sort.

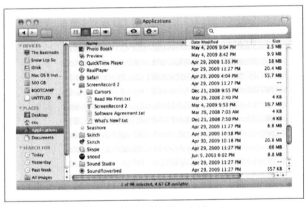

Figure 3-11. List view of the Applications folder

Column View (⌘-3)

Column View is a favorite of a lot of users. While it looks a little like List View, there are no disclosure icons to click on. Clicking on a folder in Column View reveals the contents of the folder. If you continue all the way to a file or application, the last column will show a preview of the file and give you the More Info button, which you can click to explore the selected item's metadata. For example, if you drill down to a movie, the film's preview will appear in the last column, and you can even start playing it. Figure 3-12 shows Column View.

In Column View, the arrow keys work exactly as you would expect, moving the selection either up, down, left, or right. Holding Shift while using the up or down arrow keys allows you to select multiple items in the same directory. You can change the width of the columns by dragging the two vertical lines at the bottom of the dividers between columns. Hold Option as you drag to resize all columns at once.

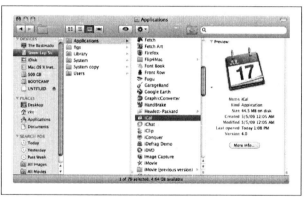

Figure 3-12. Column view of the Applications folder

Cover Flow View (⌘-4)

Cover Flow View first appeared in Leopard, and it is very slick. If you use iTunes, an iPod Touch, or an iPhone, you are familiar with Cover Flow View, as shown in Figure 3-13.

Cover Flow View gives you a graphic representation of the items in the directory as large icons. You can adjust the size of the Cover Flow area by dragging the three horizontal bars just under the previews. Snow Leopard will resize the icons to accommodate the window size. In Cover Flow View, the up and left arrow keys move the selection up in the list below the Cover Flow areas, while the right and down arrow keys move your selection down the list below the Cover Flow View area.

Figure 3-13. Cover Flow View

Common Finder tasks

You'll end up using the Finder in Snow Leopard for many basic tasks. You want to rename a folder? You'll use the Finder. Copy files? The Finder is your best friend. Move files? You will be using the Finder for that trick. Following are some common tasks you'll likely use the Finder for, and how you can get it to do what you need it to.

Rename a file, folder, or drive

Simply click the icon of whatever you want to rename and press Return or Enter. The name will be highlighted and you'll be able to type the new name. Hit Return or Enter once more to make the name stick.

Create a folder

To create a new folder, you can either choose New Folder from the Finder's menu bar or you can press Shift-⌘-N. The new folder will appear as a subfolder in whatever folder you are currently using. For example, hitting Shift-⌘-N in your Home folder results in a new folder in your Home folder. New folders are named untitled folder.

Quickly look inside a file

You can get a pop-up preview of a file's contents by using *Quick Look*. In the Finder, select the file, and press Space or ⌘-Y. An easy-on-the-eyes window will pop up displaying the contents of the file.

While Quick Look is visible, click a different file and Quick Look will look into that file. Switch Finder windows and the item in the Finder window will be displayed with Quick Look. Quick Look is file savvy; look at a Word document and you'll see what's written on the page, look at a spreadsheet and you'll see rows and columns, look at a movie and the movie will start playing. All this without having to resort to opening the program associated with file. Figure 3-14 shows a Quick Look preview.

Make an alias

There are times you want access to a file or folder without having to burrow through directories just to get at it. Some people's first inclination is to move the item to a more accessible location, but the best solution is to make an alias. An alias acts just like the regular file or folder but it points to the original. Put something in a folder alias and it ends up in the original (target) folder. Delete the alias and the item it refers to is unaffected. You can spot an alias by a curved arrow in the lower right corner of the icon. To create an alias, select the file and choose File→Make Alias (⌘-L). Then drag the alias to where you want it to be.

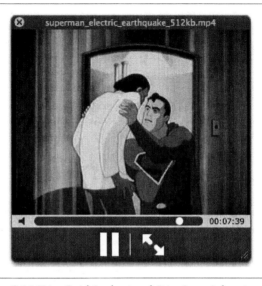

Figure 3-14. Using Quick Look to watch Brian Jepson's favorite movie

Duplicate files and folders

> If you want a copy of a file or folder, click the item you want to duplicate, select File→Duplicate, and Snow Leopard will generate a brand new copy of the selected item with the word "copy" appended. Your original item will remain untouched while you hack away at the copy.

Copy files to a new location on the same disk

> The default behavior for dragging files in Mac OS X is to move files that are on the same disk to a new location without making a copy. To copy files to another location on the same disk, hold Option while you drag the files to the new location. Once you release the mouse button, the original file(s) stay in their original location, but you get a copy in the destination location.

> The default behavior for dragging files from a location on one disk to a location on another is to *copy* them, not move

them. Hold the command (⌘) key while you're dragging the files to move, not copy, them.

Eject a drive or disk

If you've got external drives hooked to your Mac, at some point you'll want to eject them. Just yanking the drive out is a bad idea; if there is data still being written to the drive you might lose it. When it comes to ejecting drives and disks, you have options. The classic way of ejecting a drive on a Mac is to drag it to the Trash (the icon changes from the Trash icon to an Eject icon). You don't have to drag the icon to the Trash to eject it, you can eject it directly from the sidebar. That triangle next to the drive icon is the Eject symbol. Click the icon to eject it.

Snow Leopard makes the process of ejecting drives more helpful. If a drive won't eject, Snow Leopard will report what application is using files on the drive and prevent you from ejecting it.

If you want to remount a drive that you left plugged in, you can remount it with Disk Utility (*/Applications/Utilities/Disk Utility*), or you can disconnect it from the Mac and reconnect it.

Reformat a disk

If you've got a new disk, it might come in a format you don't want to use. Most flash drives and many pocket drives come formatted as FAT32 disks, but some arrive unformatted. Your Mac prefers the Journaled HFS+ file-system, and if you do not need to share files with another operating system (such as Windows), this is your best choice. To erase the drive and format it as Journaled HFS+, head to */Applications/Utilities/Disk Utility*. After Disk Utility is open, select the disk you want to format in the list of disks on the lefthand side of Disk Utility. Click the Erase tab and select the formatting you want to use for the new disk. Formatting erases all the information on the disk.

Compress files and folders

If you're going to be burning a bunch of data to a disk or if you just want to save some disk space, you can compress files and folders. There is an easy way to pull this off. Select the file with a right-click or Control-click. Select Compress from the pop-up menu and Snow Leopard will create a copy of the item with the same name, but with the suffix *.zip* appended. The space savings are variable; compressing a QuickTime movie (*.mov*) offers much less space savings than compressing a folder full of text files.

Duplicating Optical Disks

DVDs and CDs are getting less popular for sharing files due to the availability of cheap flash drives, but they are still common enough that you might need to make back up copies of important data. If you have a desktop Mac, you could install two DVD drives and copy DVDs and CDs disk-to-disk, but that is only available on high-end Macs (although you could use an external USB drive with other Macs). No worries, though; with Disk Utility you can easily duplicate that DVD and CD and burn it to a different disk.

Fire up Disk Utility (*/Applications/Utilities/Disk Utility*) and select the CD or DVD you want to copy from the list of disks in the lefthand list of available disks. Click the New Image button in the top of the window and choose DVD/CD master from the Image Format pop-up menu. Click Save and Snow Leopard will make an image of the DVD for you. Make sure you choose a location with sufficient disk space.

Once the copying operation is complete, you will have a perfect copy of the DVD or CD on your drive. How can you get that perfect copy back onto a disk? If you want to burn copy onto a blank CD or DVD, select the disk image from the list on the left side of Disk Utility

---

(if it's not there, drag the disk image from the Finder into the list). Click the Burn button and insert a blank disk when prompted. This approach will not work for copy-protected software or movies.

The Dock

The Dock is a key aspect of Mac OS X; it contains shortcuts to frequently used applications, folders, and documents. The Dock also shows you which applications are running by placing a blue dot under running applications. You can use the Dock to switch between active applications; just click the icon of the application you want to switch to in the Dock and that will become the frontmost application. An application that is starting up will bounce in the Dock so you can tell when it is loading. If an already running application begins bouncing, that is the Dock's way of telling you the application wants your attention. A typical Dock is shown in Figure 3-15.

Figure 3-15. A typical Dock

There are some items of interest here. The Finder is on the far right side of the Dock and it will always be running. Moving left to right you'll see application aliases, a divider, the Application stack, the Documents stack, the Downloads stack, a minimized window, and the Trash.

Since the Dock is conveniently located, it is a natural way of launching your most-used applications and documents. The obvious question is how can you add items to the Dock? The process is simple: just locate the application or document you want to add to the Dock and drag it to the Dock. The Dock will only let you put applications on the left side of the divider and any documents you want to add will have to be put on the right side of the divider. Even if you haven't placed an application or document in the Dock, it will appear there as long as it is running or open.

You can arrange items in the Dock by clicking and dragging them in the order you want them (dragging a running application that you haven't added to the Dock will add it). Note that adding items to the Dock does not move or change the original item, and adding (or removing) items from the Dock does not delete them.

NOTE

If you want to try to force a particular document to open in a specific application, drag the file onto the icon for the desired application (in the Finder or Dock), and it will generally try to open the file (the behavior isn't always obvious: drag something onto the Mail icon and it becomes an attachment in a message).

Once your Dock is fully loaded with applications and documents, what is there can get a little confusing. The Dock can help you out if you forget what that minimized window is or what application will start if you click that incomprehensible icon. Simply hover you mouse over the Dock item in question and a text bubble will pop up telling you what the item actually is, as shown in Figure 3-16.

Figure 3-16. Forget what application an icon refers to? The Dock has your answer!

At some point in the future you are going to fall out of love with something in the Dock and wish to rid yourself of it. Removing items from the Dock is easy; you can either click and drag the unwanted item off of the Dock (dragging it over the Trash will reveal a pop-up message saying Remove from Dock) or right-click or Control-click the item in question and click Options to reveal a pop-up menu with a Keep in Dock option (a checkmark means it will stay in the Dock even if you quit). The original item remains unaffected.

NOTE

While the Dock is generally customizable, there are two things that you can't change. The Finder will always be at the far left of the Dock and the Trash will always be at the far right. You can't move them and you can't put anything on the far sides of them. Think of the Finder and the Trash as two bookends that expand to accommodate all the items in between.

Dock Exposé

Snow Leopard has added quick access to Exposé (see "Exposé" on page 94) for a selected application. The implementation of Exposé in the Dock is very slick. Pick any running application, click and hold its icon in the Dock, and you'll get something like what is shown in Figure 3-17.

When you invoke the Exposé functionality from the Dock, you'll see all the open windows of an application at once. Any application windows that have been minimized will show up as an even smaller version below a subtle dividing line. Clicking on any window brings that window to the front. You'll also see a menu that lets you Quit or Hide the selected application, as well as an Options menu to let you keep the application in the Dock, set it to open each time you log in to the computer, or show the application in the Finder. There's a key command for this: ⌘-Tab-↑.

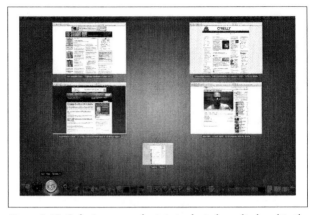

Figure 3-17. Safari's open and minimized windows displayed in the new Exposé functionality of the Dock

Dock menus

Every item in the Dock also has a Dock menu. To access this menu, right-click or Control-click the icon in the Dock. What shows up in the Dock menu depends on what you click. Application Dock menus will typically have relevant commands. For example, you can mute iTunes, skip songs, set their ratings, and so forth. All application Dock menus have these options:

- Options→Keep in Dock (if you love it, keep it in the Dock!)
- Options→Open at Login (saves you a trip to the Accounts Preference pane)
- Options→Show in Finder (this reveals where the application resides on your system)
- Hide (hides all of the Application's windows, equivalent to ⌘-H)
- Quit (you will still be warned if there are any unsaved changes)

The Dock menu for a Stack (e.g., the Applications, Documents, or Downloads Stacks) offers a different set of choices. (The following section has more details.) The options are consistent for any Stack, and feature the following:

- Sort options (Name, Date Added, Date Modified, Date Created, Kind)
- Display (Folder or Stack)
- View Content Options (Fan, Grid, List, Automatic)
- Options→Remove from Dock
- Options→Show in Finder
- Open *Foldername*

Stack view options

You've already noticed the jumble of icons in the right side of the Dock; these are called Stacks, which are representations of folders. Instead of a folder enclosing the icons, the icons are stacked like cards. You can choose which view to use for each stack; see "Dock menus" on page 72 to find out how. Here are how the available options appear:

Fan View
> If you click on a Stack in this mode, it will fan out, making it easy to choose the item you are looking for, as shown in Figure 3-18.

> Fan View is nice when there aren't a lot of items in a Stack; however, when there are more than a dozen or so, Fan View becomes less effective. If you use the arrow keys, you'll note that a blue highlight appears behind the currently selected item. Hit Return to open the item.

Grid View
> In Grid View (Figure 3-19), not only do you get to browse by icon, you can use the arrow keys to highlight an item. If the item is an application or document, hitting the Return key starts the application or opens the document. If the selection is a folder, hitting the Return key opens up another Grid View window to view the contents. It looks slick and is fun just to play with.

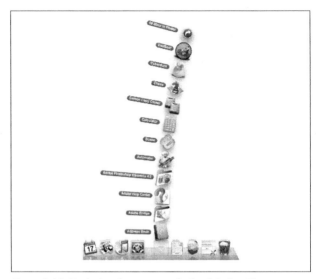

Figure 3-18. Exploring the contents of a Stack in Fan View

List View

List View (Figure 3-20) got a bit of an upgrade in Snow Leopard. Instead of the boring list on a white background, your options are now displayed as a list on the same background used by Grid View. Even with the new background, List View is a bit pedestrian compared to Fan View or Grid View, but that doesn't mean it is useless. You can scroll through the list using the up and down arrows, and when you run across a folder, using the right arrow key opens a submenu with the enclosed items.

Automatic View

If you don't feel like fine tuning the display of a Stack, you can let Snow Leopard pick the view for you based on the contents of the Stack. To get Snow Leopard to make this difficult decision for you, right-click or Control-click the Stack and choose Automatic from the "View Content as" section of the pop-up menu.

Figure 3-19. The excellent Grid View

Trash

It doesn't matter if you've got a relatively tiny SSD drive in a MacBook Air or 4 terabyte of hard disk space in a fully tricked out Mac Pro. Sooner or later, you are going to want to get rid of some files either because your drive(s) are feeling cramped or because you just don't want the data around anymore. When you find something you don't want on your Mac (for whatever reason), you'll need to use the Trash.

The Trash is located on the far right of the Dock (if you've moved the Dock to the left or right of the screen, it will be on the bottom). From the Finder, drag any files you want to banish into the Trash. Alternatively, you can highlight the item you want deleted and use the key combination of ⌘-Delete.

When the Trash has something in it (it could be one item or a million), the icon changes from an empty mesh trash can to a

Figure 3-20. List View, boring but useful

can stuffed with paper. The files you have moved to the Trash are still there, and you can retrieve them until you empty the Trash.

Open the Trash by clicking on its Dock icon. You can view the items in the Trash with any of the Finder view options, but you won't be able to actually open a file that is in the Trash (attempting to do so will result in an error message). If you find something in the Trash that shouldn't be there, you can drag it out of the Trash to save it from deletion, or click File→Put Back to put it back where it was originally.

To permanently delete items in the Trash, choose the Empty Trash option under the Finder's Application menu (Finder→Empty Trash), right-click or Control-click the Trash icon in the Dock, and choose Empty Trash, or (in the Finder) use the keyboard shortcut Shift-⌘-Delete.

Note that emptying the Trash doesn't completely remove all traces of the files. Those files can be recovered with third-party drive recovery utilities, at least until the disk space they previously occupied has been written over with new data. To make it harder for people to recover deleted data, Mac OS X includes a feature to securely delete the items in the Trash. Click Finder→Secure Empty Trash to overwrite the deleted files multiple times. If you work with a lot of sensitive files, you can make the Trash always write over the file you want deleted by going to the Finder's Preference (Finder→Preferences or ⌘-, while in the Finder) and checking the box next to Empty Trash Securely under the Advanced button. You probably want to leave the "Show warning before emptying the Trash" option checked, because once you securely empty the Trash, you're not getting that data back.

Dock preferences

Here are a few quick and easy changes you can make without invoking the Dock's Preference pane (for more information, see "Dock" on page 121). If you right-click or Control-click on the divider (it looks like a dashed line) between the section of the Dock reserved for Applications and the section reserved for files, you'll get a pop-up menu (shown in Figure 3-21) that will allow you to choose whether to automatically hide the Dock when not in use, change the magnification, change the position of the Dock, change the minimization animation, and open Dock preferences.

Figure 3-21. A quick way to make Dock adjustments

You can change the size of the Dock by left-clicking on the dashed line and dragging the pointer up or down to increase or decrease the size of the Dock.

The Application Switcher

The Dock is the most obvious way to switch between applications while they are running, but it isn't the only way. Mac OS X also features another method of switching applications and your hands don't have to leave the keyboard. It is called (unsurprisingly) the Application Switcher and it is a huge timesaver if you find yourself switching between applications often. To use the Application Switcher (shown in Figure 3-22) just hit ⌘-Tab.

Figure 3-22. Hands on the keyboard and you're still switching applications!

Hitting the Tab key (while you are still holding the ⌘ key) will cycle through open applications left to right (Shift-Tab to go right to left) and wrap around to the first application when the last application icon is reached. Alternatively, you can use the arrow keys (left and right) while holding ⌘ to move between applications. When the application you want to switch to is surrounded by a white border, release the keys and that program will come to the front.

Standard Window Controls

All windows in Mac OS X share some commonalities. Understanding the shared characteristics of windows in Mac OS X will help you be much more productive when using Snow Leopard. Figure 3-23 shows the Snow Leopard standard window controls.

Here are the controls visible in the window (the topmost group of controls are part of the *title bar*):

1. From left to right: close (red; shows an x when you hover over it), minimize to the Dock (yellow, shows a –), maximize (green, shows a +)

2. Proxy icon: drag this to create an alias of the file or copy it (hold down Option as you drag it

3. Filename

4. Scrollbars and scroll arrows to move around the document

5. Resize handle to resize the window

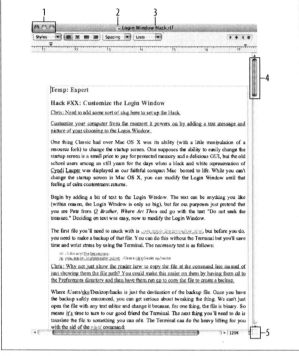

Figure 3-23. Standard window controls in Snow Leopard

Table 3-1 shows some keyboard shortcuts that are useful for working with windows.

Table 3-1. Quick application window tips

Open a new window	⌘-O
Close the active window	⌘-W
Minimize the active window	⌘-M
Minimize all windows for the frontmost application	Option-⌘-M
Cycle through the windows of an application	⌘-`

Files and Folders

Folders are where you keep your files, but Mac OS features two special kinds of folders: the Burn folder and the Smart folder. Here's how to work with each kind of folder:

Regular Folders

The Mac comes preloaded with some folders that are appropriate for commonly saved files (Documents, Pictures, Music, and so on) but you will want to make your own folders. For example, you might make a subfolder for all your spreadsheets in the Documents folder or a folder on your desktop where you can toss all those files that seem to end up on the desktop. To create a regular folder in the Finder, you can either choose File→New Folder (Shift-⌘-N) or right-click or Control-click on a blank spot in a folder and choose New Folder from the Context menu as shown in Figure 3-24.

New folders are given the default name of *untitled folder* and this name is iterated (untitled folder, untitled folder 1, untitled folder 2, and so on) if you create a series of new folders without renaming them after you create each one. To change the name, click on the folder once and then press Return or click on the folder's title. The area surrounding the title will be highlighted and you can start typing the new name in. Once the folder has been renamed to your satisfaction, hit the Return key and the name will stay with the folder until you change it.

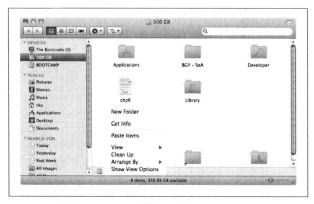

Figure 3-24. Creating a new folder via the Context menu

Burn Folders

If you've got some files or folders you want to save on an optical disk (CD or DVD), creating a Burn folder is the easiest way to get the data from your Mac to the plastic disk. To create a Burn folder, go to the Finder and select File→New Burn Folder. A new folder with a "radiation" symbol embedded in it will show up in the current folder. Be sure to give the file a nice, descriptive name like *discoinferno*. If you have made filename extensions visible (see "Finder preferences" on page 59), you'll notice that folder's suffix is *.fpbf*. Now you can start tossing any files you want burned onto the disk into that folder. The files aren't being moved to the Burn folder, they are just being aliased. When the time comes to actually burn the data, Mac OS X will burn the original file. Since the files are aliased, if you decide you want to get rid of the Burn without burning the data, you can just toss the folder in the Trash, and the original items will remain untouched.

Once you are ready to burn the data, open the Burn folder and click the Burn button in the upper-right corner. Insert a disk when prompted.

Smart Folders

There are Smart folders all over your Mac. You see them in iTunes, Mail, and even in the sidebar of the Finder. Smart folders are really searches that Spotlight performs, but that you can browse just like a regular folder.

In the Finder's sidebar, you'll note some folders with gears on them in the SEARCH FOR section. Those are Smart folders; they search your Mac for files that meet a specific set of criteria.

To create your own Smart folders, head to the Finder and choose File→New Smart Folder or press Option-⌘-N. You'll get a new window where you'll be able to set up your own Smart folder. Type in the text describing what you want to find in the folder and Snow Leopard will fill the folder with items that meet your criteria.

There isn't anything special about that; it's just a search, right? Smart folders can go much farther than a simple search like that. Clicking the + button (it is right next to the Save button on the toolbar) brings up another bar for filtering your search further.

Things get very interesting when you click on Kind. You'll get the menu with a few standard choices, but if you choose Other, you'll get a massive array of filtering options. Want to sort your songs by bitrate? It is in there! Interested in all photos taken with a certain white balance setting? Mac OS X provides that filter. You can generate amazingly refined and precise searches with Smart folders.

Two more great things about Smart folders? You can save them: just hit the Save button and you'll get a window asking where you want the Smart folder saved. The other great thing? Smart folders are constantly updated, so when you add a new file that fits the Smart folder's criteria, the file will show up in your Smart folder right away.

Nonessential But Useful Mac OS X Features

There are some feature of Snow Leopard that are really useful, but not strictly required for day-to-day use. Some people never use Dashboard, while others can't get by without it. Spotlight is fantastic for searching your Mac, but some people never search their Mac because they have insanely good organizational skills. Spaces can make that 13-inch laptop screen seem as big as you want it to be and Exposé lets you see everything on your desktop at the same time. That's a lifesaver for those who work with multiple windows, but eschewed by the user who only operates with one window at a time. If you are interested in one or more of these features, this is place to look.

The Dashboard

That speedometer-like icon in your Dock is Dashboard. Dashboard is an environment where mini-applications, called widgets, run. Click the Dashboard icon in the Dock or use the dedicated keyboard button (F4 on some Macs) and your desktop will suddenly take on a gray hue and all your installed widgets will come into view. Once the Dashboard is up and running, the widgets will go about doing whatever they are supposed to be doing (reporting on the weather, displaying a calendar, and so on). To get back to the desktop, click on a blank space in the Dashboard or press the Dashboard key again. Apple includes several widgets by default (click the + button at the lower left of the Dashboard display to add any of these). They are:

Address Book

Lets you search your Address Book from the Dashboard.

Business

Lets you search the Yellow Pages online. If you're looking for something specific, clicking the triangle on the left side of the widget will reveal a drop-down menu with commonly searched for choices.

Calculator

This is a basic calculator; much less powerful than the Calculator application built-in to Mac OS X. If you want a more powerful widgetified calculator, you can find one at Apple's Widget repository (*http://www.apple.com/downloads/dashboard/*).

Dictionary

This gives you the same information (without the Wikipedia browsing capabilities) as the Mac OS X Dictionary application. You can use the widget as a Dictionary, Thesaurus, or an Apple Help interface.

ESPN

Fetches scores and news about your favorite teams.

Fight Tracker

Lets you track flights in real time. If your spouse or roommate is returning from a business trip, you can see how long you have to clean up the house by tracking their flight.

Google

Allows you to start a Google search in the Dashboard, and opens the results in your default browser.

iCal

Lets you view iCal events in convenient widget form.

iTunes

Lets you control iTunes from the Dashboard.

Movies

Keeps you up to date on the movies playing in your area. Initially it will just cycle through the posters of currently playing movies but when you click on it, it will display showtimes and theaters.

People

Performs a White Pages search; type in the name of the person you are looking for and the People widget will take care of the rest!

Ski Report

Like to ski? The Ski Report widget will keep you updated on the conditions at your favorite slopes.

Stickies

This is the Dashboard version of Stickies. Jot down a note here and it will be on the desktop version of Stickies as well.

Stocks

Got some stocks? Track the roller coaster ride of investing in the market with the Stock widget.

Tile Game

If you had a pre-OS X Mac, you might remember the Tile game that came as a Desk Accessory. This is a widgetized version. Instead of a picture of the Apple logo, you get to unscramble a picture of a Snow Leopard. The animation when the tiles are scrambled is worth watching, even if you never actually play with the widget.

Translation

Translate a word or phrase from one language to another. The shorter the phrase, the more accurate the translation.

Unit Converter

Shouldn't everyone be using SI units by now? Well, probably, but they don't. With the Unit Converter widget, you can discover how many liters there are in an Imperial gallon.

Weather

Track the upcoming weather with this widget. You only get to choose one city to track, so if you want to know the weather in more than one place when using the dashboard, you'll have to have multiple Weather widgets running.

Web Clip

With Web Clip, you can make your own widget!

World Clock

This is a clock. If you're using Dashboard all the time and you don't have a watch or want to know the time in

Geneva while you're in San Francisco, the Clock widget is the answer to your cries for help.

Personalizing widgets

You can't personalize every widget, but you have to personalize some (for example, the Weather widget). To set preferences for a particular widget, look for a lowercase italicized *i* somewhere on the widget (usually, but not always, in the lower left-hand corner of the widget).

Adding and removing widgets

In the lower left corner of the Dashboard, you'll see a + symbol inside of a circle. Clicking this will reveal a line of widgets installed on your Mac on the bottom of the screen. If you see a widget you want to add, drag it off the bar to the location you want it to live on the Dashboard. You can overlap widgets and have multiple instances of the same widget, so if you're not careful it can get confusing quickly.

If you want to get a widget off your Dashboard, the easiest way is to hold Option, hold the mouse over a widget, and click the large white X that appears in the upper-lefthand corner of the widget. That will take the widget off your Dashboard (you can add it again later). If you want to get rid of a widget forever, you'll either need to travel to the folder where the widgets are stored and delete it by hand or use the Widget Manager included with Dashboard.

To exert more controls over widgets, use the Widget Manager. Click the X in the lower left of the Dashboard window, and click the Manage Widgets button that appears. A widget (of course) will pop up, giving you the chance to disable individual widgets by unchecking the box next to them. A disabled widget won't be available from the widget bar until you re-enable with the Widget Manager. Third-party widgets get a deletion circle next to them; if you click the –, you'll be asked if you want to move the widget to the Trash.

Getting more widgets

If you want more widgets (likely, as the widgets Apple includes are great, but there is a whole world of widgets out there), the best place to go is Apple's index of widgets at *http://www.apple.com/downloads/dashboard/*. If you have the Widget Manager up, you can also click the More Widgets button. You'll be amazed at the number of widgets available. Most are free, but some will set you back a few bucks.

Making your own widgets

There are a ton of widgets available for download, but even with all the choices available, there's a chance that the widget you desire doesn't exist. You could write your own widget to rectify the situation—after all, widgets are just snippets of code—or you could take the easy way out and create your own by using a web clip. For example, imagine you wrote a book and want to keep up with the sales ranking at Amazon. You could go to Amazon all the time and scroll down to the ranking, but that takes too much effort. Why not create your own web clip/widget to take care of the data retrieval for you?

Open Safari and surf to the information you want your web clip to retrieve. Use Safari's File→Open in Dashboard feature and a white box will appear that lets you surround the information you want your web clip to keep constantly updated with. Hit Return and your new widget will show up in Dashboard.

Searching with Spotlight

Spotlight works by indexing all the files on your Mac according to the file's *metadata* and contents. If you type "Lake Monsters Stole my Thursday" into a document, that bit of data will be available to Spotlight. Since Spotlight is the master of searching, the moment you type "Lake Monsters Stole" into Spotlight's search field (click the magnifying glass icon at the right of the menu bar to start searching), you'll start getting matching files. By the time you've typed the entire string into Spotlight, the document you typed it into will be the top result.

About Metadata

Metadata is information about a file, including the obvious, such as date created and file type, as well as a lot of unexpected information. An image, for example, contains information about the its size, the pixel count, and much more. Spotlight is smart enough to realize that when you're searching you are most likely searching for a particular filename or specific file contents, as opposed to more esoteric metadata. While Spotlight indexes everything, you won't be burdened by informational overload when performing a Spotlight search.

Controlling Spotlight's ordering of results

You can adjust how Spotlight results are ordered by opening Spotlight's Preference pane (System Preferences→Spotlight→Search Results or choose the Spotlight preferences at the bottom of a Spotlight search) and dragging the categories into your preferred order.

Controlling the results Spotlight displays

If you don't want your Spotlight search results cluttered by results from categories you're not interested in, go to System Preferences→Spotlight→Search Results and uncheck the box next to any categories you find less than compelling. Be aware that not returning results from categories doesn't mean the files aren't indexed (read on for how to control *what* Spotlight indexes).

Controlling what Spotlight indexes

There are some things you just don't want indexed. Your private plans for complete world domination, your Pog value spreadsheet, and so forth. To keep the things you want private out of Spotlight's index, go to System Preferences→Spotlight and click the Privacy tab. Clicking the + button brings up a file browsing window where you can select what you want Spotlight to exclude from the index. You can exclude entire disks or folders. Unfortunately, you can't exclude a single file, so if you're trying to keep one file out of the index you'll either have to exclude the entire enclosing folder or move that file into its own folder that you exclude.

Spotlight key commands

After you have used Spotlight a few times, you'll likely decide Spotlight is one of the better features of Mac OS X. If you're a keyboard junkie, the only problem will be how to use Spotlight more and keep your hands off the mouse. Spotlight has a nice set of built-in key commands, as shown in the following table:

Key command	Action
⌘-Space bar	Opens Spotlight menu
⌘-Return	Opens Spotlight's first result after searching
⌘-up arrow	Jumps to first result in previous category
⌘-down arrow	Jumps to first result in next category
⌘-mouse click	Opens the Finder to the folder that contains the result you clicked
Control-up arrow	Moves to first item in Spotlight menu (if you have Spaces enabled, the Spaces shortcut keys may override this)
Control-down arrow	Moves to last item in Spotlight menu (if you have Spaces enabled, the Spaces shortcut keys may override this)
⌘-Option-Space	Opens a Spotlight search window

Managing File Info

Spotlight works by indexing metadata. What if you want to add some metadata so Spotlight can find files or folders with greater precision? The Info window is your key to adding metadata (and changing much more). To open a Get Info window, select the item in the Finder and select File→Get Info (or press

⌘-I). Once you open the Info window, it will look something like Figure 3-25.

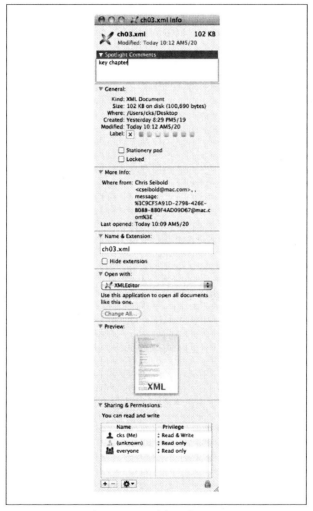

Figure 3-25. Get Info is a very useful window

There are several subsections of this window.

Spotlight comments

At the top of the Info window is a place to add Spotlight comments. Anything typed in the Spotlight comments area will be indexed by Spotlight and used when searches are performed with Spotlight.

General

You can discover some pertinent data about the file under the General disclosure triangle.

You can also turn the file into a Stationery pad by checking the box. Once you check the Stationery pad box, the file turns into a read-only file. Read-only means that you can look at it and save it as a new file, but you can't save the file with the same name as the Stationery pad. This effectively turns the file into a template. Checking the Lock button will lock the file. A locked file is much like a Stationery pad, except you can't easily throw it away. You'll get warnings when you move a locked file to the Trash, and again when you try to empty the Trash.

More Info

Clicking the More Info disclosure triangle reveals where the file originated if it wasn't created on your Mac. In Figure 3-25, the file happens to be one I emailed to myself.

Name & Extension

The Name & Extension disclosure triangle lets you rename the item and hide its extension (check the box). You can also change the extension, but that will (likely) change which program opens the file. If you change the extension, you'll get a warning from Mac OS X.

Open With

The Open With section of the Info window is surprisingly powerful. You can set the application you want to open the particular file you're looking at or you can change what programs open any file with the same extension. Clicking the popup menu will reveal suggested choices, but if you don't want to trust Mac OS X's advice, you can select Other to force an application to open a certain file type.

Preview

Preview is just the same preview of the file you would see when using the Finder.

Sharing & Permissions

Sharing & Permissions allows you to fine tune access to the file. The visible options concern your account, an unknown account, and everyone. Those are usually enough, but if you really want to control who can and can't mess with a particular file, clicking the + button will bring up even more options, as shown in Figure 3-26.

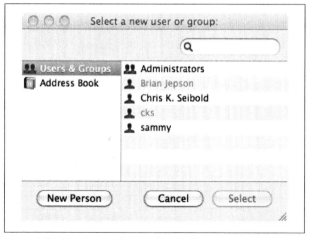

Figure 3-26. Fine tuning who can share a file

In the Select a new user or group window, you can grant access to specific individuals. Note that adding someone new (from your Address Book, for instance) will bring up a dialogue for you to set a password for the item and will add a Sharing account to your Mac for them. Adding a new group of people will add a new Group account.

Finally, if you've made a bunch of changes to sharing and thought better of it, you can click the Gear icon and you will be allowed to undo what you have wrought by selecting Revert Changes.

NOTE

The Sharing & Permissions section also has a lock icon. If you're logged in as a Standard user, you can click this to unlock prohibited features, such as the Change All button under Open With. You'll need the username and password of an administrative user to do this.

Exposé

Exposé is the answer to multiple window confusion. The idea behind Exposé is simple: instead of digging through overlapping windows, you can click a button (F3 on many Macs) and Exposé will reveal all your windows as thumbnails. Click the window you want (or use the arrow keys) and that window will move to the front.

Exposé can do more than give you an easy-to-navigate window full of thumbnails, it can reveal your desktop. To hide all those pesky windows and get to your desktop, click F11 (MacBook users will have to use Fn-F11). If you have a multitouch trackpad, you can swipe downward with four fingers to invoke Exposé; swipe upward with four fingers to show the desktop.

Snow Leopard differs from the previous version of Exposé in that minimized windows are also included when Exposé is activated. Minimized windows show up below a dividing line and are smaller than open windows on the desktop.

You can configure Exposé in the Exposé & Spaces Preference pane or, if you want to rely on the defaults (Exposé is always available so you don't have to enable the functionality), you can use the following key commands:

Key command	Action
F9 (Fn-F9 on MacBooks)	All windows become thumbnails
F10 (Fn-F10 on MacBooks)	Creates thumbnails of the front most (active) application's windows
F11 (Fn-F11 on MacBooks)	Pushes all windows aside revealing the desktop
Arrow keys	Moves between windows while Exposé is active
Tab/Shift-Tab	Moves between applications and their windows while Exposé is active
Space bar (or Enter)	Activate tshe selected window
esc	Exits Exposé

Spaces

During a typical day your Mac's desktop can get cluttered. You might have a NeoOffice window open, an iTunes window floating about, a Safari window for browsing the Web and an iMovie open while you make some last minute edits on your vacation movie. You're thinking, "Thank goodness for Exposé," but there is a better (and complementary) solution: Spaces.

Spaces allows you to create additional desktops devoted to application windows. After Spaces is configured (by default Spaces is off), you'll be able to have, for example, a desktop dedicated to Safari, another dedicated to iTunes, and yet another dedicated to iMovie (up to 16 different desktops). Sound great? Get started by turning Spaces on. To enable Spaces, head to the Exposé & Spaces Preference panel (System Preferences→Exposé & Spaces) and click the Spaces tab. Figure 3-27 shows the Spaces Preferences.

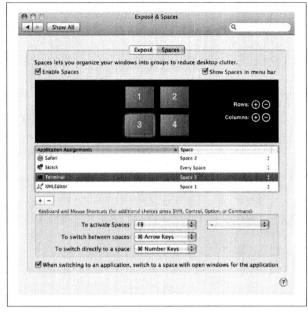

Figure 3-27. Enabling Spaces

Configuring Spaces

Once you've got the Spaces Preference panel open, you'll notice you can assign particular applications to particular Spaces. To assign an application to a Space, hit the + button. This will bring up a menu with the applications in your Dock. Select the application you want to use (if it isn't in your dock, select Other, and browse until you find the application you are looking for) and the application will be added to the Application Assignments area. Adjust the Space the application shows up in with the arrows under Space.

Using Spaces

Now that Spaces is all set up, you can switch between Spaces by using Control-arrow keys or, if you can keep track of which

Space is which number, using Control-number key to go directly to that Space.

You can also activate Spaces (F8 or Fn-F8 is the default) to show an overview of all the desktops at once. If you want to move a window to a different Space, you can drag the window to the Space you want them to show up in. Spaces takes some time to get used to, but once you are familiar with it you'll wonder how you got through the day without it.

CHAPTER 4

Quick Guide to Troubleshooting Mac OS X

Mac OS X is a robust operating system; while problems are rare, they do show up from time to time. Since these problems always seem to present themselves at the worst possible moment, it helps if you're pre-armed with the best ways to troubleshoot them. Troubleshooting is what this chapter is about, and a great reason to keep this book in your pocket!

Common Problems

There are a lot of things that can go wrong with your Mac. Hardware problems, software glitches, and configuration issues can happen at any moment. Most of the problems you'll encounter with your Mac can be easily addressed or diagnosed by following the steps in this chapter. If the information doesn't resolve the problem, it could be unique and a trip to the Apple Store or a call to Apple is in order.

Misbehaving Applications

One of the most common problems on a Mac is an application that isn't behaving as expected. The problem comes in many forms: an application that unexpectedly quits repeatedly, an application that simply stops responding, or even an application that just doesn't perform the way you expect it to.

An application stops responding

One of the problems you may encounter when using your Mac is an application that's not responding. When this happens, the application will simply stop reacting to anything. Your mouse or trackpad will still work, other programs will be fine, but if you want to use the troublesome program all you'll get is a spinning beach-ball cursor (instead of the mouse pointer) and you'll have no way to input anything.

Don't panic; there is an easy fix. Simply right-click or Control-click on the stalled application's icon in the Dock to bring up its Dock menu. If you see a message at the top of the menu saying Application Not Responding (the message is in light text), you'll also see an option to Force Quit the application. Select Force Quit (Figure 4-1) and Mac OS X will kill the program.

You may need more than one way to kill a program, because occasionally a program can become unresponsive without Mac OS X realizing that the program is in peril. For these times, launch the Force Quit Applications window either by selecting Force Quit from the Apple menu or using the key combo Option-⌘-esc. You can also try holding down Shift as you click

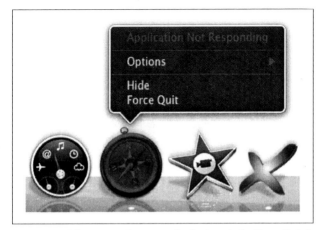

Figure 4-1. When an application isn't playing nicely, Force Quit is your best option

the Apple menu, then select Force Quit *application name* to force quit the frontmost application.

WARNING

Force quitting destroys all the data since your document (or whatever you were working on) was last saved. Some applications can recover some of your work even if you haven't saved it, but don't count on that. For example, in Safari, you can choose History→Reopen All Windows From Last Session to reopen the windows you had open.

An occasional hang is one thing, but if you find an application consistently freezing, a little more research is in order. One possible remedy is to delete the preferences file. You can find the preferences for an application in your Home folder under *Library/Preferences*. Drag the file or files associated with the troublesome application (they usually have the application's name somewhere in the preferences filename) from the Preferences folder into the Trash and restart the application. Don't

worry, the program will still work and will build a new preference file (though you will lose any preferences you have set up
for the program and will have to reconfigure them). If the application starts working, it means that your preferences file had
become corrupt somehow.

The finder stops responding

The Finder is just another program; it can get hung up. If that
happens, either get to the Force Quit item in the Apple menu
or rely on the key combination ⌘-Option-esc. If nothing happens, try clicking the Dock or some other application first, then
use the Apple menu or ⌘-Option-esc to invoke the Force Quit
dialogue.

NOTE

While every other application is forced to quit, the
Finder is *relaunched*. Why the change in nomenclature?
Unlike every other application, the Finder will be restar-
ted immediately after it is forced to quit.

Force quitting greedy processes

Turns out that the Force Quit menu doesn't show all the applications running on your Mac. If you suspect something is
eating up too much processor time or too many system resources (your Mac might be running really slowly or the fans
may be running at full speed for no obvious reason), Force Quit
won't help you figure out which application is hogging the resources. You won't be forced to restart to get your old Mac
back; instead, open Activity Monitor (*/Applications/Utilities/
Activity Monitor*), click the CPU tab, and look for any processes
that are using a lot of CPU resources for more than a few seconds (Safari and its helper applications occasionally do this,
particularly with runaway Flash or JavaScript code). With the
suspect identified, single-click on the renegade process, followed by a click on the big red Quit Process button in the

---

upper-righthand corner of the Activity Monitor window (you can't miss it, it's shaped like a stop sign).

USB device problems

It seems like computers never have enough USB ports, so most of us end up using USB hubs (or using keyboards that have extra USB ports). Then we plug some fantastic new USB device into the hub and it doesn't work. In fact, if you dig through System Profiler (it's located in the /Applications/Utilities folder) and look at the USB Device Tree (click USB from the list on the left), the hub shows up, but not the device.

Often the problem is because the device requires a powered USB port and you're using an unpowered hub (or you've maxed out the power capabilities of the hub or USB port). Switching to a powered hub instead of an unpowered one might fix the problem, but it isn't guaranteed. What works most often is plugging the device directly into your Mac, which means you'll need to shuffle the way you plug USB devices into your Mac. If any of the devices you use can run off of their own external power supply rather than taking power from the USB port, that may help as well (sometimes the external power supplies are sold separately; check with the manufacturer of the device you are using).

The second method of attacking USB device problems is a little more involved. Shut down your Mac and unplug all the USB devices (if any of the devices use external power, unplug them, too). Reboot your Mac, then plug them back in one at a time while looking at the USB Device Tree (it is updated quickly so you'll see each device as it is plugged in) to see which device isn't playing nicely with others. Sometimes going through this procedure results in all of the devices suddenly working.

If a USB device isn't working, you may need to install a new driver for it. Check the manufacturer's website for updates.

NOTE

Some USB devices, such as a GPS or other device that behaves like a serial port, rely on a chipset from a different manufacturer than the maker of the device. Two common sources of USB-serial devices are Prolific (*http://www.prolific.com.tw/eng/Download.asp*) and FTDI (*http://www.ftdichip.com/FTDrivers.htm*).

Battery problems

MacBook users are faced with a problem desktop users don't have to worry about: the battery. The goal for most Apple batteries is to still provide 80% of its original charge capacity after 300 complete charge/discharge cycles (1,000 cycles on newer MacBooks). If you're starting to notice a decreased charge time for your battery, the first place to go is System Profiler→Power (see Figure 4-2).

The Power section of System Profiler tells you the full charge capacity of your battery, how many cycles your battery has been through, and the condition of your battery. If the cycle count is getting up to the rated maximum for your battery, it is likely time to think about getting a new battery. If the cycle count is low but the battery is still running out of juice prematurely, you can try a few steps:

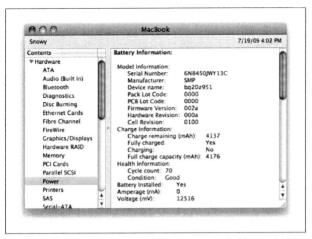

Figure 4-2. The Power section of System Profiler will tell you all about your battery

Calibrate the battery

Inside every MacBook battery is a microcontroller that tells your computer just how long it is going to last until it runs out of juice. Over time, this estimation can get farther and farther from real-world performance. To get the computer and the microcontroller on the same page, you need to recalibrate the battery from time to time. To do this, fully charge the battery and keep it plugged into the power adapter for two more hours. Then unplug the power adapter and fully drain the battery. When the warning pops on the screen alerting you to the fact that the battery is running dangerously low, save your work and keep on trucking. Let the computer sleep for more than five hours. Plug in the adapter and wait until the computer is fully charged. The battery indicator should be successfully recalibrated.

Reset the SMC

SMC is short for the System Management Controller. This chip is responsible for hard drive spin-down, sleep and wake, and backlighting. A malfunctioning SMC can prevent the battery from charging. To reset the SMC (after you have shut down your Mac) remove the battery and unplug the power adapter from the computer. Hold the power button for five seconds. Replace the battery and plug in the power adapter. Restart the computer. This won't work for a MacBook with an internal battery. For those models, shut the computer down and plug it into an adapter that is getting power. On the left side of the keyboard hold Left Shift-Control-Option and press the power button. Wait for five seconds and restart the computer.

If those remedies don't restore your battery, it is likely time for a trip to your local Apple Store or authorized repair center. If your computer is under warranty, and your cycle count is low, Apple will probably replace the battery. If your cycle count is over the recommended number, and the performance degradation is within expectations, you'll probably need to replace your battery or live with the reduced (and ever-shrinking) battery capacity.

NOTE

Like many computer makers, Apple has had its share of battery recalls. In some cases, batteries that pose a danger are recalled. In other cases, they are recalled for performance reasons. Regardless, you should check with Apple to see if your battery is under recall. It is likely that they will replace a battery under recall even for a computer that is out of warranty.

Display problems

Most Macs come with a built-in display that doesn't require special configuration, so display problems are uncommon. When they do happen, it is often user error. The fix, while usually easy, isn't readily apparent. Here are some things you can try:

Fuzzy/tiny display

If your display is fuzzy (or everything is suddenly bigger than you remember), it's possible that you or someone else changed the resolution of the display (on some systems, this may also manifest itself as a small screen with black bars around the border of the screen). Head to System Preferences→Displays and look for the monitor's native resolution (on Macs with built-in displays, this will usually be the highest resolution available at the bottom of the list). Once you select the optimal resolution, you'll be happy again.

Your display moves with your mouse

I've received several panicked calls and emails about this issue. The weird thing is that it always happens when children under five are on your lap while you are using your computer. Is there some kid detection receiver in your Mac that turns on screen moves with mouse? Of course not. What has happened is your kid has depressed some keys while you were working (if you don't have kids or lap cats, then it was probably you).

There are a couple of key combinations that will cause your Mac to zoom the screen (the most common is holding down Control while you zoom in or out with your mouse wheel or trackpad). Once you're zoomed in, your mouse will suddenly be dragging the screen around. It is disconcerting if you are not expecting it. To turn it off, hold down Control and zoom out with your trackpad or mouse wheel. There is also another sequence of keyboard commands that may be invoked accidentally: Option-⌘-8 will toggle keyboard zooming on (or off), and holding down = or – while pressing Option-⌘ zooms in or out.

Startup Problems

A misbehaving application is bad enough, but a Mac that won't start properly is truly disconcerting. The good news is that most problems are usually repairable. The general method of attack in this case is to get your Mac to a state where you can run Disk Utility and repair the drive. However, there are some situations where you can't even get to that point.

Your Mac beeps at you instead of starting

If you've got a bad memory (RAM) module, you'll need to open up your Mac and replace that module. On Intel Macs (PowerPC Macs have slightly different beeps, but they won't run Snow Leopard), these startup beeps will tell you what's up:

One beep	No RAM installed
Three beeps	RAM does not pass integrity check

NOTE

For memory-related errors, you should try installing some memory that you know is good to see if that resolves the problem. If you don't have any spare memory lying around, try removing each RAM module and replacing them one by one until you've isolated the bad memory.

If you don't know how to replace memory in your Mac, check the user guide that came with it. If your Mac is still under warranty, you can skip the manual investigation and bring it into an Apple Store for service.

Your hard drive is making noises

If you suspect a physical hard drive problem, you need to check things out quickly before they get much, much worse. A hard drive problem is often obvious if you hear a strange noise, but can also be indicated by the computer stalling for several seconds at a time (or making a clicking sound when stalling). If you've listened to the National Public Radio show *Car Talk*, you know that one of the highlights is when callers try to imitate the sounds their cars are making. Just as with a car, when a bad sound is emanating from your hard drive, it isn't usually a good thing. If you're inclined to identify the sound, head over to *http://datacent.com/hard_drive_sounds.php* and take a listen to the sounds of a dying drive, sorted by manufacturer.

WARNING

If your hard drive is failing, you are likely to lose more data every moment it is running. If you do not have current backups, your best bet is to replace the drive immediately, and either seek a data recovery professional or, if you don't have the money for that, install the damaged drive in an external drive enclosure and use the dd_rescue utility (*http://www.gnu.org/software/ddrescue*) to recover the data on the damaged drive.

If you aren't hearing any obviously unusual sounds, but still suspect your hard drive is causing your problems, head to Disk Utility and check the S.M.A.R.T. status of the drive.

S.M.A.R.T. is yet another acronym (using a computer means loving acronyms) and this time the acronym is clever, if a little forced. S.M.A.R.T. stands for Self-Monitoring, Analysis, and Reporting Technology. The idea behind S.M.A.R.T. is that many hard disk failures are predictable, and that computer users, given a heads-up that their hard drive is on the verge of failing, will be able to recover data before the failure actually happens. You can discover your drive's S.M.A.R.T status by opening Disk Utility (in */Applications/Utilities*) and selecting the disk you are worried about. In the lower right side of the Disk Utility window, you'll see S.M.A.R.T Status: you'll either see Verified (everything is fine, as shown in Figure 4-3) or About to Fail. If you get the About to Fail notice, don't waste any time; if your Mac is under warranty, take it into the Apple Store. Otherwise, back up as soon as possible and start pricing out the cost of a new drive.

Startup troubleshooting

Thankfully, the hardware failures just described are relatively rare. Much more common are software failures. Corrupt files,

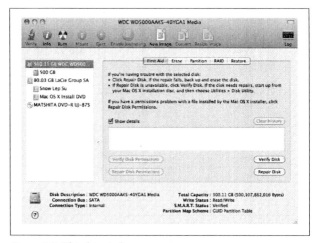

Figure 4-3. This drive is fine

wonky login items, and even font problems can cause a startup failure. These issues are generally repairable, hopefully without data loss. Unfortunately, when you have one of these problems, the cause isn't immediately obvious. When faced with a Mac that won't boot, there are a few things you can try to get your Mac back to a usable state:

Restart your Mac

A lot happens when Mac OS X starts up. It checks your Mac's hardware, prepares the system software, and more. During the startup process, there are ample opportunities for something to go wrong, especially right after installing an update to Mac OS X or even an application. If your Mac won't start, don't panic; restart the machine and chances are everything will be fine.

Safe Boot

If a simple restart doesn't do the trick, it means you have problems that persist across restarts, so the next step is a Safe Boot. In Safe Mode all startup items are disabled, font caches are cleared, and some other possibly problematic items are avoided. More important, Safe Boot gives you a chance to run Disk Utility, uninstall any software that may be misbehaving, or back up your data before whatever is causing the problem gets worse. To get your Mac to boot into Safe Mode, hold down the Shift key after you hear the startup chime and release the key when you see the spinning wheel appear. Once the Mac is booted, run Disk Utility (located in the *Utilities* subdirectory of *Applications*).

Boot from another disk and run Disk Utility

If all else fails, try starting from another disk with Mac OS X on it. If you have one, you can use an external drive with Mac OS X installed on it. Otherwise, use your Snow Leopard Install DVD or the Restore DVD that shipped with your Mac. To force your Mac to boot using the optical drive, press and hold C while starting. To choose a different drive (an external disk), hold the Option key while starting to get a list of all available startup drives.

NOTE

If you start from your Snow Leopard or Mac Restore DVD, you'll find yourself in the Mac OS X Installer. To launch Disk Utility, click the Tools menu on the menu bar and select Disk Utility.

This section emphasized Disk Utility because all Macs come with the handy program. There are several (often more powerful) disk repair programs available from third parties, such as DiskWarrior (*http://www.alsoft.com/DiskWarrior*) and TechTool Pro (*http://www.micromat.com/*).

Reset your PRAM

This troubleshooting step gets its own section only because it's one of the oldest troubleshooting techniques in Mac history.

PRAM (parameter random access memory) is where your Mac stores many of its hardware settings. Resetting the PRAM almost never resolves a startup issue, but it is something Apple support usually asks you to do when troubleshooting a problem (and it does, in some rare cases, help). To reset the PRAM, turn on your Mac, *immediately* press and hold the Option-⌘-P-R keys, and continue to hold the keys until your Mac restarts and your hear the startup chime a total of three times. If you reset the PRAM, you may have to reconfigure some of the system settings (date, time, and possibly keyboard/mouse settings if you've customized them).

AppleJack

It seems as though computer problems happen at the worst possible times. Whether this is some intrinsic law of the universe or perceptual defect common to all of us doesn't make any difference when you're on the road, especially if your Mac

---

won't start and you don't have a startup disk. With a little preplanning (and zero expense) you can add an emergency utility that will help you fix your Mac when it won't boot normally.

AppleJack works by taking advantage of a feature called *single user mode*. Single user mode is a different way of booting your Mac. Instead of the usual highly visual interface you've come to expect, single user mode gives you a command prompt and a plain text screen. Not very exciting, but single user mode only loads the very basic parts of Mac OS X, so chances are good that single user mode will work even if your Mac won't boot. Once you're in single user mode, AppleJack can repair your troublesome disk.

For AppleJack to work its magic, you'll have to take the 30 or so seconds it takes to install AppleJack. Do it now so it will be there when you need it. Head to *http://sourceforge.net/projects/ applejack* to download the program and while you're there, take a few minutes to read all about the project at AppleJack's project page: *http://applejack.sourceforge.net/*.

To start your computer in single user mode, hold down ⌘-S as the computer boots. If it's in good enough shape to start in single user mode, you'll get a shell prompt where you can type commands. To run AppleJack, type **applejack** and press Enter or Return. AppleJack can run any of the following tasks or run all of them in sequence:

1. Repair disks
2. Repair permissions
3. Cleanup cache files
4. Validate preference files
5. Remove swap files

AppleJack can be a real lifesaver if you don't have a startup disk with you and things go wrong, so it is worth your time to install it right this second!

CHAPTER 5

System Preferences

Preferences and Your Mac

Out of the box, the Mac is a fantastic machine. The graphical interface is clean and uncluttered, tasks are accomplished with a minimum of frustration, and everything performs exactly how you expect it to. That honeymoon lasts for somewhere between 10 seconds and a week. While everything is great at first, you will find yourself saying, "It would be better if...." When this happens, your first stop should be System Preferences.

Why System Preferences? It turns out that Apple knows that different people want different behaviors from their Mac. While Snow Leopard can't possibly accommodate everything that everyone might want to do, most of the changes you are likely to want to make are built right into Snow Leopard.

System Preferences, which appears as a silver framed gears icon in the Dock (unless you've removed it from the Dock, in which case you can still find it in the Applications folder), is the place to make your Mac uniquely yours. But as you'll see later in this chapter, you can find some tweaks by going beyond System Preferences.

One inevitable thing that will happen while you are adjusting your System Preferences is that you'll make a change and later decide that it was a mistake. For example, you might adjust the time it takes for your Mac to go to sleep and later decide that Apple had it right out of the box. Fortunately, many preference panes feature a Restore Defaults button that will reset the settings for that particular preference pane to factory defaults.

NOTE

You can also find System Preferences in the Apple menu.

Searching for Preferences

There are 26 or 27 preference panes (the exact number depends on whether you're using a MacBook or desktop Mac) installed with Snow Leopard. Each preference pane controls a bevy of related preferences. With all that going on, there is no way for you to remember where to find every setting: are the settings for display sleep under Energy Saver or Displays?

Snow Leopard takes away the pain of finding the right preference pane by including a search box in the preference pane window (Mac OS X is big on search boxes). Type in what you're looking for and the likely choices will be highlighted. You'll also have the benefit of suggested searches being displayed.

NOTE

When you're searching, try searching for one term at a time. For example, if you can't find the settings for putting your display to sleep by searching for "display sleep," try searching for "display" or "sleep."

In Figure 5-1, I'm searching for "alerts" so I can change the alert sound. Snow Leopard has highlighted the most obvious candidates and it is right: if I click on Sound, it takes me where I want to go.

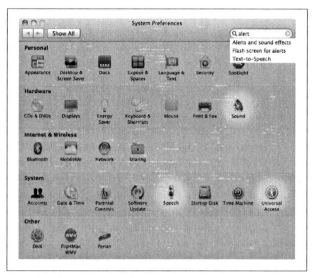

Figure 5-1. Searching for "alerts" in System Preferences

Preference Pane Rundown

With so many preference panes, it's hard to keep track of what each one does. This section goes through all the preference panes quickly.

In System Preferences, you'll find five categories: Personal, Hardware, Internet & Wireless, System, and Other. Other is reserved for non-Apple preference panes and does not appear until you've installed third-party preference panes (which usually, but not always, are part of a third-party application).

Some preferences, such as those that affect all users of the computer, need to be unlocked before you can use them (there will be a lock icon in the lower left of the window). These can only be unlocked by a user who has administrative access. On most Macs, the first user you create has those privileges. If you don't have administrative privileges, you'll need to find the person who does and have them type in their username and password to make those changes.

Appearance

Appearance lets you tweak the look and feel of Mac OS X. The first two options control two color settings. The one labeled Appearance controls the overall look of buttons, menus, and windows and has two choices: blue or gray. The one labeled Highlight controls the color used for text you've selected and has more choices.

You can also control the appearance and behavior of scroll bars and arrows, choose whether double-clicking a window's title bar minimizes it to the Dock, and choose how many items (Applications, Documents, and Servers) are available under Recent Items in the Apple menu. Additionally, you can change the font-smoothing preferences (if your Mac has an LCD monitor, it is best to leave this enabled).

Desktop and Screen Saver

The Desktop and Screen Saver Preference pane has two tabs. The Desktop tab lets you control the image you use for the desktop background (also known as wallpaper). You can use the Apple-supplied images, solid colors, or pictures from your iPhoto Library. You can even specify a folder full of images by clicking the + button in the lower-lefthand corner.

If you've specified an image of your own, you can choose how the image is displayed by selecting Fill Screen, Fit to Screen, Stretch to Fit Screen, Center, or Tile from the menu to the right of the image preview. The fun isn't over yet; if you like a little liveliness from your desktop, you can set the desktop to change the picture periodically. Apple supplies options ranging from every five seconds to every time you log in or wake from sleep.

You can also disable the translucent menu bar setting under the Desktop tab.

The *Screen Saver* tab gives you complete reign over Snow Leopard's built-in screen saver. For something as seemingly mundane as a screen saver, you can get a lot out of the Screen Saver Preference pane. Apple includes several built-in screen savers; while most are just interesting abstract animations on your screen (sadly no flying toasters), there are two that are a bit more informative than the rest. The RSS Visualizer lets you watch an RSS feed roll across the screen (to change the RSS feed displayed, click Options and change the URL). Word of the Day works exactly how you might imagine; you get a word and a definition. Since it's from Apple, it's rendered more beautifully than any other word-of-the-day thing you can imagine.

If you're wondering if you can use your pictures from iPhoto, the answer is "of course!" All your iPhoto pictures appear here; you can choose your entire library or a specific event, album, or MobileMe gallery. If you specify a collection of pictures, you can change the way the pictures are displayed. The buttons just below the preview (labeled Display Style) let you choose between Slideshow, Collage, and Mosaic. Click the Options button for more control over how the pictures are displayed on your monitor.

Can't decide on a screen saver? Let your Mac select one for you; just check the box next to Use Random Screen Saver.

Immediately under the Use Random Screen Saver checkbox, you'll find another checkbox to superimpose a clock over your screen saver. The Test button lets you see your screen in action before actually committing to said screen saver.

The Screen Saver pane also allows you to set the delay between the time you stop using your Mac and the moment the screen saver kicks in. Adjust the slider beneath the Preview window to set the delay time.

NOTE

If you make this delay longer than the delay set for your Mac to sleep, a yellow warning sign will pop up and inform you of this fact. Don't worry, nothing bad will happen. You'll just never see your screen saver because by the time it kicks in, the screen will already be blank.

If you'd like the screen saver to kick in on demand, you can set aside a hot corner to invoke the screen saver right away. In the lower lefthand corner of the Screen Saver pane you'll see a button called Hot Corners. Click the button and you'll get a new window with options for every corner. You can choose any corner you want; when you move your mouse to that corner, it fires up the screen saver (or one of the other options you've selected). Nice for when you're surfing the net and the boss walks up. The only downside of setting hot corners is that you get up to eight options for each corner, so unless you want to use a modifier key with the corner, you're stuck with more options than corners.

NOTE

If you are willing to use a modifier key (you can choose from Shift, ⌘, Option, or Control), you can get a single corner to do many different things. To add a modifier key to a hot corner, hold down the modifier key while you select what you want the hot corner to do. Using modifiers with hot corners not only gives you extra flexibility, it prevents you from accidentally invoking the hot corner action when you're mousing along.

Dock

You won't find a lot of options with the Dock Preference pane. For example, you can't control the 3-D look or change the dots that appear underneath running applications. Though some things can't be changed, you'll still get control over the most important aspects of the Dock. You can control the size of the Dock—from the illegibly small to the ridiculously large—by using the Size slider. The slider works in real time so you can see the changes as you adjust the slider. You also have the option to enable Dock magnification.

If you turn on magnification, then the application or document you're mousing over will become larger than the rest of the items in your Dock. How much larger? Use the Magnification slider to set just how big the current item of focus becomes.

You also have the ability, through three radio buttons, to put the Dock where you want it: Left, Bottom, or Right. (Top is not an option because you don't want the Dock in direct competition with the menu bar.)

The Dock Preference pane lets you choose which animations are used when you minimize a window: the Genie effect or Scale. These days the choice is really a matter of personal preference, but in the early days of Mac OS X, some machines were not fast enough to render the Genie effect.

There's also a checkbox titled Animate Opening Applications, which sounds like more fun than it actually is. All it does is control whether application icons bounce when you launch an application. If you turn this option off, you'll still be able to tell if an application is starting because the dot that appears under it (or next to it if the Dock is positioned to the left or right) will pulse.

If you select Automatically Hide and Show the Dock, it will remain hidden until you move the mouse above or next to its location.

The Minimize Windows into Application Icon option is new to Snow Leopard. If you leave this unchecked, minimized application windows will take up space on the right of the Dock (or bottom if the Dock is anchored to the left or right). With this option checked, you'll save space in the Dock, but to restore minimized application windows, right-click or Control-click an application's icon, select the minimized window from the application's window menu, or invoke Exposé.

Exposé and Spaces

The Exposé and Spaces Preference pane allows you to configure Exposé (see "Exposé" on page 94) and Spaces (see "Spaces" on page 95). You'll find two tabs in this preference pane, one dedicated to Exposé and one dedicated to all things Spaces.

In the Exposé tab, you'll find lots of options for invoking Exposé. The first section will let you set screen corners (with or without modifier keys; hold down Shift, Control, Option, or ⌘ as you click for more options) that will activate Exposé and other functions. After you've selected an option with the drop-down menu, move the mouse to that corner, and Exposé will come to life.

You aren't stuck with just using the mouse and screen corners to invoke Exposé; you are also able to assign keys and mouse buttons to invoke Exposé. You can control which key or mouse button fires up Exposé for showing all windows, application windows, or the desktop. To change the key used for any of the functions of Exposé, click the leftmost pop-up menu and choose from the options that include all the function keys, the modifier keys (left or right), and the function key (fn). Choosing the – option turns the key for that Exposé function off. To set a mouse button for an Exposé function, click the rightmost pop-up menu next to the option. Changing the buttons used to launch Exposé in the preference pane does not change the behavior of the built-in Exposé key on certain Mac keyboards.

The Spaces tab of this Exposé and Spaces Preference pane lets you enable and configure Spaces. Get Spaces running by checking the box next to Enable Spaces, and a menu extra for Spaces by checking the box next to Show Spaces in menu bar. The Spaces menu extra will present you with a list of Spaces to jump to. In the dark section of the Spaces tab you can add rows and columns to Spaces. The maximum number of Spaces is 16 (four rows and four columns).

Once you've created the number of Spaces you desire, you can control which application(s) use which Space with the next section of the tab. Hit the + button to add applications to Spaces and use the up and down triangle icon (it appears to the right of the current Space assignment for that application) to assign the application to a particular Space. To eliminate an application's settings, click the application's name and hit the – button.

Once you have all the application assignments set, you can choose how you want to activate Spaces (you can choose any of the function keys), how you want to switch between Spaces (modifier key and arrow keys), and how you want to switch directly to a Space (modifier key and the number associated with that Space).

The last option you get in the Spaces tab affects application switching. Check the box to automatically move to the Space where that application has windows open when you switch to that application using the Dock or ⌘-Tab. Leave it unchecked to stay where you are when you switch to that application (you can click the Dock icon twice to switch to a Space where it has open windows).

Language & Text

Using the Language & Text Preference pane, you can set the language used by your Mac with the Language tab. From the Formats tab, you can control the format of the date, time, and numbers, and pick which currency symbols you want to use.

The Text tab is of immediate use if you spend any amount of time typing. Clicking the Text tab opens the Symbol and Text Substitution list, which gives you the option of typing (r) and having it automatically show up as ®. Even better, you can add your own substitutions. Click the + button to add whatever text you what substituted and check the box. This won't work in every application, but in the supported applications the text substitutions can save a lot of effort.

There's more under the Text tab. You can select how Mac OS X checks your spelling (default is automatic by language, but you could have Mac OS X check everything for French even if your Mac is using English by default). You can tweak the Word Break (which affects how words are selected when you double-click on a word) with a drop-down menu and customize how smart quotes appear.

From the Input Sources tab, you can click Show the Input Menu in menu bar, which adds a multicolor flag to the otherwise grayscale menu bar. If you check the box labeled Keyboard & Character Viewer (at the top of the list of Input Sources), you'll be able to launch the Character Palette and Keyboard Viewer from the menu bar.

Security

The Security Preference pane is likely one of the most useful and most overlooked preference panes in OS X. Take your time setting up the preferences and your data will be much safer than if you stick with the defaults. Ignore the Security Preference pane and people can see more of your data than you'd like to share, particularly if they have physical access to your Mac.

The Security Preference pane features three tabs: General, FileVault, and Firewall. If you want to spend 30 seconds making your Mac much safer, the General tab is the place to visit. The first option on the General pane is labeled Require password after sleep or screen saver begins, and lets you choose Immediately, or after some other duration.

This requires anyone who wants to use your computer to enter a password if the screen saver has started or if your Mac has been asleep. This does require more typing on your part, but is likely worth the inconvenience, especially if you're using your Mac in an open setting. Not requiring a password would let anyone that walked by shake your mouse and start poking around. Unless you log yourself out every time you're away from your Mac for more than 30 seconds, seriously consider enabling this option.

The rest of the options in the General section of the Security Preference pane are for administrators only. You can click the lock and type in an administrator username and password to make changes to the following settings:

Disable automatic login
    Checking this box means all users will be required to login each time the computer is restarted.

Require password to unlock each System Preferences pane
    System Preferences can be powerful you wouldn't want just anyone mucking with them. Check this box to force any user to authenticate before changing any preferences.

Log out after X minutes of activity
    This is a little redundant if you already require a password to wake the computer or get past the screen saver, but for total control, this is a better option. You can force your Mac to log out after any period of inactivity you choose ranging from 1 to 960 minutes (that's 16 hours!). This option will attempt to shut down any applications you are running, so save your work before you wander away.

Use secure virtual memory
    When your Mac is running, it uses a portion of your hard disk (a *swap file*) for data stored in RAM that's not currently being accessed. This could be troublesome if someone gets access to your computer, since there's no telling what is in the swapfile (passwords, credit card numbers you've typed into a web form, and so on). This option

encrypts the contents of the swapfile. Changes take effect after your next restart.

Disable remote control infrared receiver

By default, your Mac (excluding the Mac Pro) will accept input from almost any infrared device. This can present a security risk and be very annoying if you're using Apple TV while you're using your laptop. Turn this behavior off by checking the box. If you want to be able to use a remote with your Mac but have it ignore all other remotes, click the Pair button and follow the instructions that appear on screen.

FileVault tab

FileVault provides an extra layer of security for your data. When enabled, FileVault encrypts your entire User folder with the Advanced Encryption Standard (AES) algorithm, the same algorithm used by governments to protect classified data. All that encryption might sound a bit hard on your Mac, and you might imagine encrypting and decrypting all that data would slow your system down. Mac OS X manages this trick on the fly and you'll never notice a substantial slow down from FileVault. The first time you enable FileVault, it can take a bit of time to set up, though.

If you decide to enable FileVault, you will need to set a master password for your Mac. This will allow you to retrieve the encrypted data if you ever lose the password associated with the account you are going to encrypt (FileVault works on an account by account basis, so you don't have to encrypt every account on your Mac). If you forget your account password and your master password, the information in the FileVault protected account will be gone forever. You can set a master password in the FileVault tab of the Security Preference pane.

Once the master password is set or ignored, clicking Turn on FileVault... brings up an window where you are asked for your account password. Once you've entered your password, you'll be presented with a window asking if you wish to securely erase your Home folder after the data has been encrypted, which makes sure no one can retrieve your data after it has been erased.

Once all the choices have been made, your Mac will log you out and encrypt the data. When it's done, you can log back in.

Firewall tab

The Firewall tab of the Security Preference pane deals with your connection to the Internet and networks. The default setting is off. This means your Mac will listen to just about anything coming over the network. Surprisingly, this is usually not a problem.

To turn on the firewall, first authenticate if needed (click the lock and type in your administrator name and password), and hit the Start button. The light next to the Firewall status entry will turn green and the firewall will be up and running.

Now that the firewall is running, you might be wondering what it is actually doing. For that information you'll have to click on the Advanced... button. After clicking Advanced, you'll get some options to have Snow Leopard's firewall perform more to your liking. The first option is to Block all incoming connections. If you check this box, then Snow Leopard will only listen to incoming connections for very specific, necessary network communications. You'll also notice that a box warning you that using the Block all incoming connections setting will prohibit you from using sharing services such as screen sharing and file sharing.

A less inhibiting option is checking the box next to Automatically allow signed software to receive incoming connections. In this scenario, software that has been signed (the author is known to Apple and Mac OS X has confirmed that it has not been altered or corrupted) is allowed to receive incoming connections. Every Apple application on your Mac has been signed, so you won't need to worry about killing any of the built-in applications. You can also add applications to the list even if they aren't signed. Click the + button and you'll be able to add other applications to the list of programs allowed to communicate.

NOTE

Since any signed application is allowed to receive connections, not seeing the application you're wondering about on the list doesn't mean that it won't be able to use the network. Instead of trying to add applications that you think won't work to the list of allowed applications, a better tactic is to wait for an application to try to connect to the network; Mac OS X will ask if you want to allow it to accept incoming connections.

In the Advanced section of the Firewall tab, you also have the option to turn on stealth mode. If you check the box next to Enable Stealth Mode, your Mac is less visible on the network. For example, should some nefarious person try to scan all ports at your IP for a way in, they'll get no response. To that person, it is like no computer exists at the scanned IP address. However, network activity you engage in, such as visiting a web page or checking your email, can reveal your presence on the network.

Spotlight

The Spotlight Preference pane has two tabs. The Search Results tab, which allows you to adjust the order of results returned by a Spotlight search (drag the items to change the order of results) and to change the Spotlight shortcuts via pop-up menus. The Privacy tab allows you to add folders to be excluded from Spotlight's search. Note that you can't add individual files to the list. For more information on Spotlight, see "Searching with Spotlight" on page 88.

CDs and DVDs

This preference pane controls what your Mac does when you insert an optical disk. Even better, you can select what happens when optical media is inserted, according to the type of optical media inserted. You get to decide what your Mac does when it detects a blank CD, a blank DVD, a music CD, a picture CD, or a video DVD. To change the behavior from the defaults, click the pop-up menu next to the type of CD or DVD you want to change and choose what you want your Mac to do.

When you click the menu, you'll see Apple's recommended choices (the audio CD menu includes Open in iTunes, for example) but you aren't limited to just the predefined options. Choosing Open other application... will bring up your Applications folder and you'll be able to choose any application you like. You can also opt to have a script run when you insert a disk. When you choose this option, you'll be presented with the familiar window that you can browse to the repository where the scripts you want to use are saved.

Displays

If you own a laptop or an iMac, you probably won't visit this preference pane until you need to connect a second monitor or projector. On the other hand, if you're a color perfectionist or need to connect your Mac to a non-Apple display, then a stop by the Displays panel is necessary. With this preference pane you can control the resolution of your monitor, set the color depth, adjust the brightness, and calibrate the color to fit your needs.

If you are using multiple displays, you can set the location of the menu bar, enable display mirroring, and also configure the spatial arrangement of each screen so they can correspond to how the displays are physically arranged.

Energy Saver

You get different options in the Energy Saver control panel based on what kind of Mac you're using. The big difference being that on a MacBook you'll get two tabs, one for Battery and one for Power Adapter. The tabs make sense on a laptop because you will likely want different settings when you are using the power adapter than when you are relying on the battery to power your MacBook. One other small difference between a desktop and laptop Mac Energy Saver Preference pane is the Show battery status in the menu bar. It is checked by default, giving you a quick way to visually assess how much time you have left to run on battery power. If you feel that the menu bar on your Mac is simply too crowded, unchecking the box will free up a tiny bit of space in your menu bar.

Although you have two tabs if you're using a MacBook and a single window if you're using a desktop Mac, the options are very similar. The slider next to Computer sleep allows you to define the delay between the time you stop using your Mac and the time your Mac enters sleep. Sleep is a low-power mode, so while your Mac is sleeping it uses much less power than when it is being actively used. The benefits of sleep over powering down your Mac include a rapid start up (waking from sleep has been quick in Mac OS X but it is even faster in Snow Leopard) and that any documents or pages you have open will be there waiting for you when you wake your Mac. As you can guess, the separate tabs (Battery and Power Adapter) on a Mac laptop allow you to set different values for when your Mac sleeps depending on your MacBook's current power source. The second slider, Display sleep, adjusts how long it takes for the Display to Sleep (turn black).

To change either of these, use the slider to set the value anywhere from one minute to never.

Under the sliders you'll get some checkboxes:

Put the hard disk(s) to sleep when possible

> This checkbox will put your drives to sleep when OS X thinks it is a good idea. Some hard drives have this functionality built-in, but Mac OS X will put the drives to sleep before the hard drive firmware would normally take over.

Wake for network access

> If you use Back to My Mac or have a copy of Apple Remote Desktop, you'll probably want to check this box. This allows your Mac to wake up when you want to log in remotely.

Automatically reduce brightness before display goes to sleep

> Checking this box means that your display will noticeably dim before it becomes completely black. Any mouse or keyboard action will bring the display back to full brightness.

Slightly dim the display when using this power source (MacBook/ MacBook Pro only)

> This option is only available in the Battery tab of a MacBook's Energy Saver Preference pane. As you can probably guess, this is an effort to extend battery life by making the display dimmer when relying on battery power. In practice, most people don't notice the difference.

Start up automatically after power failure

> Checking this box means that should the power flicker, your Mac will start up again as soon as the power comes back on. Note that your Mac isn't really aware that the power has failed to part of the grid, the system just knows that no shut down protocol was followed. If you accidentally hit the off button on a surge protector, the Mac will power back on when the button is moved back to the on position. For obvious reasons, this option is not available in the Battery tab of a MacBook's Energy Saver Preference pane.

If you're a very regular person, you can get the best of all worlds by clicking the Schedule... button. This brings up a drop-down pane where you can set a specific time for your Mac to start up or wake and a specific time for your Mac to Shut Down, Sleep, or Restart by choosing the schedule from the pop-up menu and entering a time in the box.

Sounds fantastic, right? Well, maybe the Schedule option isn't all that it could be. You have to be logged in for your computer to Shut Down at a specific time and your computer must be awake. So, it is a great option if you're sitting in front of your Mac when you want it to Shut Down, but unless you're comfortable leaving your Mac unattended and awake while you're logged in, the automatic Shut Down option isn't going to be of much use.

The problems with sleeping or shutting down your Mac automatically aren't present when having your Mac wake or start automatically; automatic start up will work exactly as you expect. For example, if you're sitting down in front of your Mac every weekday at 8:07, having your Mac automatically start up at 8:03 can save you a few minutes of waiting each day.

Keyboard

The Keyboard Preference pane is where you'll find yourself when you want to change key commands (see Chapter 9 for a list of common key commands) or change how your keyboard responds to your typing. The preference pane is divided into two tabs: Keyboard and Keyboard Shortcuts.

Keyboard tab

The Keyboard tab allows you to adjust (via sliders) the Key Repeat Rate and the Delay Until Repeat. The first slider allows you to adjust how fast a key repeats while it is being held down and the second slider adjusts how long you have to hold a key before the key starts repeating. You'll also have the option to use all the numbered F keys as standard function keys. If you check the box next to this option, those labeled keys on your Mac keyboard won't work the same way; pressing F11 won't mute your Mac, it will invoke Exposé (but you can still use the function key to get back the original behavior). You also have the option to show the Keyboard and Character Viewer menu extra in the menu bar. Checking this box puts a menu extra in your menu bar so you can get easy access to characters (arrows and such) with the character viewer and a simulated keyboard showing you what the modifier keys do when pressed.

Keyboard shortcuts

The Keyboard Shortcuts tab is where you can adjust the key commands used by your Mac. To help you find the key command you want to change, the left side of the pane has a list of applications so you can more easily locate the key command you want to change. To actually change a key command, double-click on the key command you want to change and type the key you want to use. You can use the function keys or keys with modifiers as your new choice. Figure 5-2 shows an example.

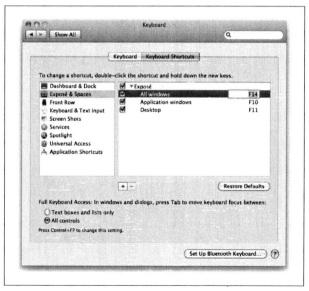

Figure 5-2. Changing the key command for Exposé

To add a key command, click the + button. You'll see a pop-up menu that, when clicked, will provide you with a list of applications that you can add a keyboard command for. Type the menu title exactly as it appears in the application's menu, and type the key you want to use for a shortcut. For example, you'll note that there is no keyboard command for customizing the toolbar in the Finder. Imagine you want to add one. Select the Finder from the pop-up menu, type `Customize Toolbar...` (with the dots) in the menu title box, click in the Keyboard Shortcut field, and type the key you want to use for the shortcut. Now when a Finder window is active, you can hit the key you chose and the Customize Toolbar window will show up. As a bonus, the key command you added will also appear next to the menu title in the drop-down menu of the menu bar. If you tire of your custom key command, click the shortcut once and hit the – key. Your key command will be banished. The Restore Defaults button will also kill your custom key command and any other changes you've made.

You'll note that there is a setting for Full Keyboard Access. Full keyboard access is a way for you to interact with your Mac without using the mouse (you'll be able to use Tab to move from field to field in most applications).

The final thing you'll notice in both tabs is the Set Up Bluetooth Keyboard option. If you've got a Bluetooth keyboard that Mac OS X isn't recognizing automatically, clicking this button will force Mac OS X to search for it.

Mouse

The Mac has been able to use multibutton mice since OS 9, but the standard configuration on a fresh install of Snow Leopard is for the mouse to behave as though it only has one button. If this isn't to your liking, a trip to the Mouse Preference pane is necessary.

Mighty Mouse options

If you're using a Mighty Mouse, you'll discover sliders to adjust tracking, double-click and scrolling speed. You'll also note pop-up menus on every part of the Mighty Mouse that can detect pushes. Each pop-up menu will let you specify the action taken when the button is depressed. You can assign a multitude of things to the button of choice, including secondary clicks and application launching.

After you are done setting up your Mighty Mouse buttons to your liking, you can control how the Mighty Mouse scrolls with the pop-up menu next to Scrolling. You turn it off, scroll vertically only, vertically and horizontally, or scroll 360 degrees.

The Mouse Preference pane will also allow you to set up your Mighty Mouse to zoom by checking the box next to Zoom. You can select the modifier key to invoke zooming when the scroll ball is being used. If you take a trip to the Options button, you'll find some settings to fine tune the scrolling done with the scroll ball.

If you're using a non-Apple mouse

Some people don't like the Mighty Mouse and that's OK, your Mac is happy to work with non-Apple mice. Some mice ship with custom drivers, but most are able to work with your Mac straight out of the box. What customization options the Mouse Preference pane offers for third-party mice depends on the model you are using.

Trackpad

Your trackpad options will depend on what MacBook you use. On newer MacBooks, those with multitouch trackpads, you'll get the options described in the multitouch section. If you have an older MacBook, you'll get a different set of options. The cutoff point is the multitouch trackpad, which was first introduced on the MacBook Air in 2008. Luckily, you won't have to worry about which trackpad you have; Snow Leopard will install the appropriate preference pane for your MacBook.

Multitouch trackpads

In the Trackpad Preference pane, you'll be able to adjust tracking, double-click, and scrolling speed using sliders. You'll also be able to configure whether the trackpad should respond to a tap. You'll find options for Tap to Click, Dragging, Drag Lock, and Secondary Click. Note that the Dragging and Drag Lock options won't become checkable until you've selected the previous option. If you're wondering just how these options work, Mac OS X provides a video showing you exactly what happens as you select the options.

You'll also be able to enable or disable options such as Scroll, Rotate, Pinch Open & Close, and Swiping. You can customize the zooming behavior of the trackpad by clicking the Options button and you can turn on or off Secondary Click (the same as a right-click or Control-click) using the checkbox.

Figure 5-3 shows the Trackpad Preferences pane.

Older trackpads

If you've got an older MacBook, you'll still have a Trackpad Preference pane but the options will be different. You'll still control Tracking Speed, Double-Click Speed, and Scrolling Speed with sliders, but you won't have options for swiping and pinching. You will discover checkboxes to allow:

- Two-finger scrolling
- Horizontal scrolling
- Zooming (with options)
- Clicking (tap trackpad to click)
- Dragging (tap trackpad twice to drag the selected item)
- Drag Lock (when you're dragging an item, tap again to release the item)
- Tap trackpad using two fingers for right (secondary) click

- Ignore accidental trackpad input; this function attempts to ignore unintended input (like resting your wrist on the trackpad while you're typing)

Figure 5-3. The Trackpad Preference pane and the instructional movie that accompanies it

Print & Fax

The Print & Fax Preference pane varies depending on how your Mac is configured. If you've got a modem attached to a telephone line, you'll see two tabs: Print and Fax. If you're not connected to a telephone line, you'll only see the Print tab.

The Print tab is where you can add printers for your Mac to use. Click the + button and an Add Printer window will open. You'll see a list of printers your Mac has access to when you click the Default button at the top of the window. Selecting one of the printers listed will allow you to change the name of the printer, set the location, and select the driver you want to use. If the driver wasn't installed when you installed Snow Leopard, Mac OS X will attempt to retrieve the appropriate driver over the Internet.

After your printer has been added, you can see what is waiting to be printed using the Open Print Queue button and, depending on the printer, check supply levels for ink. Clicking the Options button will allow you to change the name of the printer under the General tab and change the printer driver under the Driver tab. You might have more tabs depending on the model of your printer.

Using the Fax tab, you can configure your faxing preferences for any installed faxes or fax modems.

If your printer also has scanning capabilities, you'll see a Print and Scan tab to the right of the list of printers after you click on the printer in the list. Click Open Scanner to bring up a window where you can scan a document.

Sound

The Sound Preference pane is broken into three tabs: Sound Effects, Output, and Input. The output volume is always available at the bottom of the pane regardless of which tab you're using. This is also your chance to rid yourself of the Volume menu extra (that menu bar might be getting crowded). Just uncheck the Show Volume in menu bar box.

Sound Effects allows you to choose an alert sound from the listed options. To preview a sound, click it or use the arrows to move up and down. Snow Leopard gives you plenty of options for audio alerts, so hopefully you can find something to your liking.

The next question is where do you want the alert sounds to come from? If you have speakers plugged in, you can opt to send the sound through the speakers or through the built-in speaker(s) in your Mac. The drop-down menu reveals all your choices.

Immediately under the list for choosing where your alert sounds and sound effects will emanate from is a slider to adjust the alert volume. You might want your alert sounds to be softer than the rest of the sounds coming out of your Mac (you don't want Basso walking all over iTunes, right?) and this is the place to set it. It is, however, a one-way street. The maximum volume that the alert will play at is the same as the master volume for your system. If you want alerts to be the loudest noise coming out of your Mac, you're out of luck unless you can turn down the volume of other sound-generating programs.

Finally, you get three checkboxes so you get the sounds you want to hear and skip the sounds you don't. By checking the box next to each entry you can:

- Play or silence user interface sounds (an example of a user interface sound is the sound the Trash makes when being emptied).

- Play feedback when volume is changed (if you hit a volume key or move the volume slider, the alert sound will play at the newly selected volume).

- Play Front Row sound effects (you only have to worry about this when you're using Front Row, but if you don't like the sounds Front Row makes while you navigate, this is the place to kill them).

The next tab of the Sound Preference pane is the Output tab. In the first tab, you were able to decide which speakers played alert sounds. With the Output tab you get to decide where everything else is played. For example, you could choose between your Mac Pro's internal speaker (not great for that lusted immersive media experience) or the top-of-the-line speakers you plugged in to the optical out port to hear the sweet sounds emanating from iTunes. Headphones are a special case, as plugging headphones in kills the internal speakers.

You also might get some extra options depending on your hardware. For example, if you're using the built-in speakers on an iMac or MacBook, you get to adjust the balance with a slider under the window to choose which side gets the greater burden.

The Input tab is where you control your Mac's "ears." If you're using anything but a Mac Mini or Mac Pro, your Mac has a built-in microphone. It is called the Internal Microphone, and it is the default selection for sound input. This means that any audio chats, video chats, or podcasts you record will get recorded via the Mac's built-in microphone. If you want to use a USB microphone, plug it in and select it from the list.

Your other choices in this window are Input Volume. This controls how "hot" (as they say in the radio business) the sound coming into your Mac will be. Turn it all the way up and you'll have those you're chatting with reaching for their volume controls a millisecond into the conversation.

There is a final checkbox for Ambient Noise Reduction. Checking this box tells your Mac to ignore the sounds going on around you—screaming kids, howling wolves, what have you. It isn't perfect, but it helps out when you're chatting or, more important, using voice commands with your Mac.

MobileMe

If you're a MobileMe subscriber (a free trial comes with a new Mac or you can go to *http://www.apple.com/mobileme/* to try MobileMe for 60 days at no cost), this preference pane is where you can set up MobileMe to work for you. With MobileMe, you can sync your data to the MobileMe service (and in turn, you can sync to other Macs, iPhones, or iPod Touches). MobileMe also includes iDisk, which lets you store lots of data on MobileMe's servers. For more information on MobileMe, see Chapter 7.

Account tab

In the Account tab you have two options: Sign Out... and Account Details. Sign Out... signs you out from the service. If you sign out, the entire preference pane turns into a chance to Sign in or a chance to read the sales pitch for MobileMe. Your other option in the Account tab is to click Account Details. Clicking this takes you to the Internet where you can manage your MobileMe account with Apple's easy-to-use interface.

Sync tab

This tab allows you to set the schedule for syncing your computer to MobileMe. Checking the Synchronize with MobileMe box let's you choose the frequency of syncing. Your options are the usual suspects (hourly, daily, weekly) plus two more interesting options: Automatically and Manually. If you opt for Manually, MobileMe won't sync until you click the Sync Now button. Choosing Automatically tells MobileMe to sync as often as necessary and results in the most frequent syncs.

Once you've made those choices, you can choose what you want to sync. MobileMe provides a long list of syncable stuff ranging from bookmarks to preferences. Sync the items you want and MobileMe will take care of the rest.

Clicking the Advanced... button brings up a list of computers registered with MobileMe and the last time they were synced. It also gives you the option of removing a no longer used computer (click the machine you no longer want to sync and click Unregister). You also get the opportunity to Reset Sync Data. Clicking that button allows you to replace selected (or all) data on MobileMe's server with the data from the selected computer.

iDisk tab

The iDisk tab gives you a quick visual way to see how much room you have left on your iDisk, as well as a chance to buy more (the Upgrade Storage button). You also get some options for your iDisk's public folder. By default, anyone can go to the public folder of your iDisk and grab any file stored within. If you want people to be able to also store files in your public folder, click the "Allow others to write files in your public folder" checkbox. Check the "Password-protect your public folder" checkbox to require a password for people who connect to your public folder.

iDisk Sync is very useful if you use your iDisk with regularity. Your iDisk is stored somewhere in Apple's cloud of servers. With iDisk sync you can treat it almost as a local disk. Once you choose to turn iDisk sync on (click the Start button), your iDisk will show up as a mounted volume. You can add and remove files as you see fit, even if you're not connected to the Internet. Once you reconnect, iDisk will sync the data in your local iDisk drive with the data from your online iDisk. This behavior can sometimes cause file conflicts. There's an option to have iDisk always favor the most recent copy of a file when resolving conflicts.

Back to My Mac tab

If you have MobileMe, you can use Back to My Mac. With Back to My Mac enabled, by clicking the Start button your Mac will be accessible from any other computers using your MobileMe account. Just look in the sidebar of a Finder window and you'll see the computers you can access. If your router doesn't support NAT-PMP (Network Address Translation Port Mapping Protocol) or UPnP (Universal Plug and Play), Back to My Mac will not be able to automatically configure your router.

Network Preference Pane

This pane allows you to configure your network. You can set up an Airport, Bluetooth, Ethernet, or FireWire connection.

Sharing

The Sharing Preference pane allows your to share a variety of files and allows others to share bits of hardware over your Network:

DVD or CD Sharing
> This option allows other computers to use the optical drive in the host Mac. There's a checkbox to have your Mac ask you before anyone accesses your Mac's optical drive.

Screen Sharing
> Allows other computers to view your screen and control your computer over the network. You can specify which

users are allowed to connect, or specify that all users are allowed. If you'd like to allow people to connect from non-Mac computers, click Computer Settings and enable the VNC (Virtual Network Computing) option. They will need a VNC client such as RealVNC or TightVNC.

File Sharing

File Sharing allows others to access your shared files over your network. It's a nifty way to trade files. If you turn this option on, make sure you created a nice password.

If you have enabled file sharing, users on other computers have a few ways to connect. If the computers you want to share files between are on the same local network, they can get to your computer by choosing Connect to Server from the Go menu of the Finder's menu bar. The address needed to access the computer will be your Mac's name with *.local* appended.

It may be even easier, though. Mac OS X features a zero configuration networking protocol named *Bonjour*. You'll see other computers that you can access in the sidebar of a Finder window.

Users will have to supply a username and password to connect. You may want to set up a sharing-only user (see "Setting up accounts" on page 34) for this.

If you want to access your files from another Mac while away from your home or work network, check out Back to My Mac in "Back to My Mac" on page 185. Click the Options button to enable printer sharing for people using Windows computers, and also to turn on FTP file sharing.

Printer Sharing

Checking this box turns your Mac into a print server. If you're on a laptop and want to print something in the basement, you won't have to haul your carcass over to the printer or even send the file to the Mac hooked to the printer for later printing. Just check the Printer Sharing box on the Mac hooked to the printer and you can print from anywhere on you Local Area Network.

Scanner Sharing

This is Printer Sharing's less-used little brother. It works in much the same way; if you've got a scanner connected to the host Mac you can use it from a remote computer. This feature is new in Snow Leopard.

Web Sharing

This isn't the box to check if you want to share your Internet connection; this is the box to click if you want to share web pages in your Sites folder. Turning Web Sharing on reveals a URL for your computer's websites and your personal website (which happens to be the computer's website with ~username appended) that people on your local network can visit. Once you turn on Web Sharing, the preference pane shows the addresses where your site's folder and computer can be reached. The URLs will be something like **http://yourcomputername/** and **http://yourcomputername/~yourhomefoldername**.

Configuring this to allow people to connect over the Internet is possible, but for home and many office users, you'll need to configure port forwarding on your router to allow outside traffic into your network. Your website will be available over Bonjour networking as well; you can configure Safari to display Bonjour sites in its bookmarks by open Safari's Preferences and going to the Bookmarks pane.

Remote Login

This allows users to connect to your Mac over SSH (Secure Shell). To connect using SSH, you'll need to open a Terminal window (*/Applications/Utilities/Terminal*) and either use the *ssh* command-line utility or select Shell→New Remote Connection.

Remote Management

You'll need Apple Remote Desktop to use this. If you have a copy of Apple Remote Desktop and want to use it to connect to your Mac, make sure this box is checked.

Remote Apple Events

Checking this box will let other Macs send Apple Events to your Mac. What are Apple Events? They are wide ranging, but just about anything AppleScript can do can be an Apple Event.

Xgrid Sharing

Xgrid allows intensive computing tasks to be broken up and worked on by individual Macs. This option is mainly used for scientific research and other processor-intensive tasks.

Internet Sharing

Internet Sharing allows you to share your Internet connection with other computers. You can choose to share a wired connection via Airport or an Airport connection with another computer wired to yours. If you are sharing a wired connection via Airport, you can choose to add some security measures.

Bluetooth Sharing

Checking this box allows Bluetooth devices to interact with your Mac. You can customize your Mac's behavior when receiving files, designate a folder for the files your Mac accepts over Bluetooth, set up browsing behavior, and designate which folders users can browse on your Mac.

Accounts

Using this preference pane, an administrator can manage accounts (you'll need to authenticate first). To add or delete accounts, use the + and – buttons immediately under the list of users. For a complete discussion of managing accounts, see "Accounts" on page 31.

Clicking Login Options gives you the ability to enable or disable automatic login. You'll also get to choose how the Login window appears, Name and password is more secure than List of users because anyone trying to get into your Mac will need to guess both your username and password.

You'll also have the option to show the Restart, Sleep, and Shut Down buttons on the login window, show the input menu in the login window, show password hints, and the option to use VoiceOver at the login window.

Finally, you can enable Fast User Switching. Fast User Switching allows you to switch between accounts without logging out of an account. You'll still need a password to get back to your account, but if an application was running when you switched users, it will be running when you come back to your account. The View as menu gives the option of viewing users by name, short name, or icon. For more information on Fast User Switching, see "Logging In" on page 40.

Date & Time

The Date & Time tab allows you to set the date with the Calendar interface (or just type it in) and set the clock. You can also check the box next to Set date & time automatically and choose your server (where your Mac fetches the current date and time from) in the menu to the right. You can modify your date and time formats by clicking the Open International button, which will take you to the International Preference pane.

The Time Zone tab sets the time zone you want your Mac to use. You can let your Mac try to find your location automatically or manually set it. If you set it manually, you'll have to click on the map or provide the name of a major city in the same time zone.

The Clock tab gives you the option of showing the time in the menu bar, allows you to choose how the time is displayed in the menu bar, and lets you tweak a few other options.

You also have the option to have your Mac announce the time from every quarter hour to every hour. If you click the Customize Voice button, you'll get options to change the voice used to announce the time, the volume used to announce the time, and even the rate at which the time is announced.

Parental Controls

Parental Controls is Mac OS X's way to protect your kids while they are on the Internet. Some people may want to sit beside their kids while they access all that the Web has to offer, but for many people the direct supervision option simply isn't feasible. The Parental Controls Preference pane takes some of the worry out of allowing a child to use the Internet unsupervised by setting a variety of rules and filters. These control not only where your child can go on the Internet but what programs they can use and even who they can chat with and email.

NOTE

While Parental Controls is set up for kids, you can manage any user who is not an administrator with Parental Controls.

Parental Controls is an encompassing preference pane, so there are a lot of options. To avoid overwhelming you, Parental Controls has five tabs.

System tab

The System tab allows you to enable a simplified Finder for those who are unable to grasp the vagaries of the regular Finder and to control which applications the user can run. If you're enabling content controls, controlling which applications the managed user can run is essential.

To select the particular applications your managed user can run, click the box next to Only allow selected applications and use the triangles to expand the program list and check the applications you choose. Other options are presented with their own checkboxes and you can choose to allow the managed user to burn DVDs, administer printers, change their password, and modify the Dock (all of these apply only to their account, not to any other accounts on your Mac).

Content tab

The Content tab gives you the option of hiding profanity in OS X's built-in dictionaries (just click the checkbox), but the bigger draw is the ability to manage web browsing.

Website Restrictions, the section of the Content tab concerned with where people can go while they are on the Internet, offers three levels of control, each enabled with a radio button.

Allow unrestricted access to websites
> Clicking this radio button allows complete access to the Web.

Try to limit access to adult websites automatically
> If you check this button, Mac OS X will rely on filters and lists of adult websites and try to block them. It is surprisingly accurate. The downside is that the filter also blocks all https (secure) websites. If your teen is doing online banking, he or she won't be able to access their account. If you want to add an allowed site or specifically exclude a site that isn't caught by the filter, click the Customize button and add sites that you approve of and block sites you don't want your kids visiting. You can grant access to specific https websites in this way.

Allow access to only these websites
> This is the most restrictive option. The sites a managed user can visit are limited to the ones preinstalled by Apple or ones you have entered into the list by clicking Customize below the radio button. To add or delete sites, use the + and – buttons.

Mail & Chat tab

This tab limits who the managed user can interact with via email and iChat. You get the option (via checkboxes) to control Mail, iChat, or both. Once you've checked the box, any person you want your kids to be able to email or chat with will have to be entered either manually by hitting the + button and typing in their email address and instant messaging information, or by selecting their information from your Address Book (click the triangle button to open the Address Book).

Time Limits tab

The Time Limits tab allows you to set a maximum amount of time the computer can be used per day and when. Just drag the sliders to the amount of time you want the user to be able to use the computer on weekdays and weekends. You can limit when the user can use the computer by adjusting the time in the Bedtime section.

Logs tab

If you've gone through the trouble of setting up Parental Controls, you might wonder if you're getting any return on your investment of time. Clicking the Logs tab will reveal where your kid has been going, has tried to go, and gives you access to their iChat transcripts. See something you don't like? Hit the Restrict button at the bottom of the page and add the website or chat participant to the group of blocked sites or individuals.

Software Update

The Software Update Preference is focused on getting updates for Mac OS X and telling you which updates you have already installed. There are two tabs in Software Update.

Scheduled Check tab

Scheduled Check allows you to set up a schedule for checking with Apple servers for new updates. Uncheck it and you'll have to check for updates manually. You also have the option to automatically download updates. This can be useful because as soon as an important update is downloaded (automatically, behind the scenes) you'll be notified and can install it without having to wait for the download to complete. Note that Software Update only updates Apple software.

Installed Software tab

The Installed Software tab gives you a list of all the updates you've installed on your Mac.

Speech

If you have ever seen Star Trek, you've probably dreamed of talking to your computer and having the machine do your bidding by voice only. Mac OS X can do that. Getting the most out of Speech will require some tweaking, though. The Speech Preference pane has two tabs, Speech Recognition (the exciting "control your Mac with your voice" stuff) and the more mundane Text to Speech tab, which gives you a good deal of control over how your Mac reads text.

Speech Recognition tab

The Speech Recognition tab has two subtabs, Settings and Commands. Both tabs allow you to turn Speakable Items on or off. The Microphone menu allows you to choose which microphone to use. You can choose any microphone plugged into your Mac or go with a built-in microphone (assuming your Mac has one). The Calibrate key opens a window where you can practice giving your Mac verbal commands. The Change Key button lets you change which key you press to tell Mac OS X to start listening. The next section allows you to have the Mac listen only while the key is pressed or listen after you speak a keyword. If you decide to go with a keyword instead of a button, you can choose whether the keyword is optional and if it is required before or after the command. The default keyword is *computer* but it is probably wiser to go with a word that you don't say when frustrated (as in "stupid computer").

Rosebud works well, just don't watch *Citizen Kane* while computing. There's also an option for the computer to play a sound to acknowledge that it has received your command. To get an auditory response, check the box next to Upon Recognition and choose the sound you want to hear.

The Commands tab of the Speech Recognition tab is where you control just what speakables are allowed. The Select command set gives you a list of choices. You can turn a particular set of commands on or off by checking the box next to the one you wish to use. Highlighting any choice will bring up a short explanation of what your commands will control.

The Open Speakable items folder will pop open, as shown in Figure 5-4. This is the folder where all your installed speakable actions are stored. You have a bevy of choices built right in and you can always create your own.

Figure 5-4. A small sampling of speakable items for Mail

Text to Speech tab

The Text to Speech tab gives you control over how Mac OS X reads text back. It also lets you decide if you want to hear an announcement when an alert is displayed or when a running application needs your attention. To control what voice your Mac uses to read text, select your favorite from the menu next to System Voice. Control the speed at which the text is read using the Speaking Rate slider. For a little fun, select Show More Voices from the System Voice menu and test them out. Most voices say something different and there is often some humor in the test.

Startup Disk

Startup Disk allows you to specify which currently attached disk you wish to use to start your Mac. You can use any valid startup disk (valid choices will show up in the window) including DVDs and external disks. Clicking Restart... reboots your system using the selected disk as the startup. You can choose your disk while your Mac is starting by depressing and holding the Option key.

If your Mac has a FireWire port, you can also choose to start the machine in Target Disk Mode. This turns your high-priced Mac into a glorified hard drive, but is extremely useful for transferring data, preferences, and repairing troublesome hard disks.

Time Machine

Time Machine is Apple's answer to the annoyance of backups. With this preference pane, you can choose where to back up, what to back up, and when to back up. For more information, see "Time Machine" on page 173.

Universal Access

Universal Access is designed for those with some impairment that prevents them from using their Mac in a standard manner. But it's also fun for anyone who wants to use their Mac in a nonstandard manner.

When you select the Universal Access Preference you'll note that there are four tabs: Seeing, Hearing, Keyboard, and Mouse. You'll also notice that the text is bigger and bolder than the standard preference pane. Each tab controls a different method of interaction with your Mac. Across all the tabs you'll have checkboxes for enabling access for assistive devices and an option to add a Universal Access menu extra to your menu bar.

Seeing tab

When the Seeing tab is selected, you'll see radio buttons to turn VoiceOver on or off. VoiceOver is the built-in screen reading utility for Mac OS X. You'll also find buttons for enabling screen zooming on your Mac. If you want to customize the behavior of your Mac when zooming, click the Options button. You'll also find radio buttons allowing you to change the display to either Black on white or White on black text. If you want to eschew color altogether, check the box next to Use grayscale (this is also a great way to simulate a retro computing experience). The Enhance Contrast slider will bump up the contrast, making subtle things harder to see while making text easier to read.

Hearing tab

In the Hearing tab, you can choose to have the screen flash instead of having your Mac use an audio alert. This can be quite useful when the volume on your Mac is muted, so don't hesitate to try it out. You'll also find an option to play stereo audio as mono.

Keyboard tab

For some, pressing the various keystrokes needed to operate a Mac can be challenging. Sticky Keys, the first option in the Keyboard tab, solves this problem. Instead of being forced to hit multiple keys (such as ⌘-P) at the same time, sticky keys will force your Mac to interpret ⌘ followed by P as ⌘-P. You'll also find checkboxes that allow you to turn Sticky Keys on or off with five taps of the Shift key, a checkbox to enable beeping when a modifier key is pressed, and an option to display the pressed keys on the screen as you are pressing them.

If you have trouble with keystrokes, you can enable Slow Keys. This puts a delay between when a key is pressed and when it is accepted. With this option, for your Mac to recognize a key press, you'll have to press the key and hold it for a period of time. That period of time is adjustable with the Acceptance

Delay slider. You'll also find radio buttons to enable click key sounds (your Mac will make a sound when a key is depressed and a different sound when the key is accepted).

Mouse tab

For those who have trouble using a mouse, Mac OS X can let you control the mouse cursor with the keyboard. You can turn this behavior on or off in this tab, and control the delay before the keyboard starts controlling the cursor. You can also specify the maximum speed of the cursor via the slider found in the Mouse tab. If you have trouble seeing the cursor, you'll also find a slider to change the size of the cursor.

Non-Apple Preference Panes

Non-Apple preference panes show up in the Others category. In fact, the Others section of the preference pane won't show up until you add an application that has a preference pane. These preference panes work the same as Apple's own preference panes; they allow you to control some aspect of a program or feature you added. For example, if you install Perian (*http://www.perian.org*), your Mac can display a greater variety of video types. The only direct interaction you can have with Perian is through its preference pane.

One of the most common questions about third-party preference panes isn't how to use them; it's how to get rid of them. If the third-party application doesn't include an option to uninstall its preference pane, you can manually uninstall third-party preference panes by right-clicking or Control-clicking the preference pane you want to remove and selecting the Remove option (see Figure 5-5).

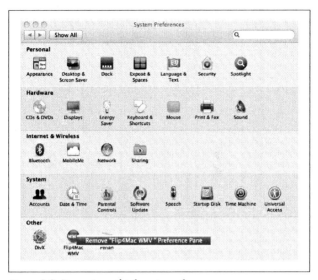

Figure 5-5. Removing a third-party preference pane

CHAPTER 6

Built-in Applications and Utilities

Snow Leopard comes with a bevy of useful applications. After installation, you won't be left with just the operating system; you'll get an image editing program (Preview), a word processing program (TextEdit), a chat application (iChat), and a lot more. Installing Snow Leopard also installs must-have applications like Safari for browsing, Mail for all your email chores, and iChat AV for carrying on conversations with your friends. You also get some applications that are just plain fun. You can easily kill an afternoon playing with the backgrounds in PhotoBooth, and Front Row makes watching movies or looking at photos a truly engaging experience on your Mac. The Mac OS X version of Chess can give most players a serious challenge.

Not as routinely useful, but just as important in the long run, are the utilities included with Snow Leopard. Activity Monitor sounds painfully dull, but when you're trying to figure out which application is misbehaving, it is a lifesaver. Likewise, taking shots of your screen may seem like the pinnacle of mundanity. Yet, sooner or later, you'll want to take a snapshot of your screen and share it, and you'll be glad Snow Leopard comes with a utility called Grab.

Applications Installed with Snow Leopard

Following are all the applications installed by default with Snow Leopard. Note that the list only covers applications installed with a Snow Leopard install. If you have a brand new Mac or are upgrading an older Mac, you'll likely have applications (such as iLife) that are not included in the list.

Address Book

Address Book keeps track of all your contacts' information—everything from phone numbers to email addresses. You can customize entries, so adding and deleting fields is no problem. To change the label for a field or add a completely new field for a contact, just click the Edit button at the bottom of the card. The best thing about Address Book is that it is integrated throughout Mac OS X. You'll be able to access your contacts in Mail, iChat, and even some third-party applications.

Your Address Book data can be synced with MobileMe, mobile phones (using iSync), and iPods/iPhones (using iTunes).

NOTE

When you set up your Mac, Address Book will automatically add an entry for you. That might seem crazy. After all, you know how to get in touch with yourself, but there are benefits: for example, you can drag your card from Address Book into an email to send it to anyone you wish.

Automator

Automator is a workflow tool for automating repetitive tasks: resizing a bunch of photos, converting filetypes, combining text files, syncing files between folders, and so on. Just about anything you can do with your Mac, you can automate. What's even better is that there is a good chance there is already an

Automator script ("action") for the task you are trying to complete. Not only does Automator come with a bevy of useful scripts already installed, but the Web is replete with premade examples. See *http://www.apple.com/downloads/macosx/automator/*. Don't forget, the real fun is creating your own Automator actions.

In Snow Leopard, Automator is also the first destination when you're creating services you'll be accessing from the Services menu. See the sidebar "The Services Menu" on page 48 for more details.

Calculator

When you fire up the Calculator application you get a basic calculator. If you explore the Calculator's menu bar, you'll note that Calculator has built-in conversion functions, scientific and programmer modes (on the View menu), and numerous conversion functions (on the Convert menu). If you want a history of your calculations, you can get a running record by using Paper Tape (⌘-T). Calculator is also speakable, meaning that the program can read both button presses and the results if you want it to; just visit the Speech drop-down menu in Calculator's menu bar.

NOTE

Using Calculator for basic math isn't the fastest way to get the answer. Spotlight has the functions of Calculator built-in, so if you need a simple expression calculated, type the question into Spotlight (see Figure 6-1) and skip Calculator altogether! At the end of the year you can invoke Calculator to estimate how much time this tip saved you.

Figure 6-1. The same answer as Calculator, but much more convenient

Chess

Fancy a game of chess? If so, Mac OS X has you covered. Predictably, you get the standard human versus computer chess game (with adjustable difficulty), but you also get four chess variants, a tweakable board and pieces, and the ability to speak to your Mac to move your pieces. You can also pit the computer against itself or play against another human. Sadly, you can't play chess against someone over a network, so if you want a head-on challenge with a human, they'll have to be at your Mac with you. Anytime you want to save your game just hit ⌘-S.

Dashboard

The Dashboard application icon in the Applications folder simply invokes Dashboard. It's much easier to do with a mouse button or trackpad shortcut (see "Mouse" on page 134 or "Trackpad" on page 135), a key command (F10 or F4, depending on your Mac), or the Dock icon. If you don't want to use the Dock, you can drag the icon for Dashboard off of the Dock. If you want the icon back, just drag it back to the Dock from the Applications folder. Dashboard is covered in detail in "The Dashboard" on page 84.

Dictionary

This is the dictionary responsible for Mac OS X's system-wide spell check. The application also lets you search a thesaurus, Apple's dictionary, and Wikipedia. You can choose which of these four options to use, or search them all at the same time. In many applications, highlighting a word followed by a right-click will open a menu that allows you to look up that word with Dictionary.

DVD Player

DVD Player plays (surprise) movie DVDs. Unlike Front Row, you can use DVD Player to play a movie in a window while you're doing something else on the computer. DVD Player adds many options you don't get with Front Row, such as tweaking the color or messing with the audio equalizer. If you've got an Apple remote laying around, you can use it to control DVD Player.

NOTE

By default, DVD Player fires up the movie in full screen (you can change this behavior by selecting DVD Player→Preferences). Move your mouse to the bottom of the screen to access the playback controls, move it to the top of the screen to select chapters from the DVD, and to the very top of the screen to reveal the menu bar where you can select the size of the playback window.

Font Book

Font Book gives you control over all the fonts on your Mac. Snow Leopard installs over 100 fonts by default and other programs will install even more. You can preview, group, install, and deactivate fonts using Font Book. Font Book is also happy to validate your fonts to identify any damaged fonts that can

---

cause your system to become unstable (the Validate option is found in Font Book's File menu).

In some cases, duplicate copies of fonts can cause programs to be unstable. Font Book will let you deactivate duplicate fonts: Select Edit→Select Duplicated Fonts, then select Edit→Resolve Duplicates.

Front Row

When you want an immersive media experience on your Mac, Front Row is there. Watch movies, listen to music, look at pictures, and more. Just about any media you want to access is available to Front Row, even the media on your other Macs. Invoke Front Row by using an Apple remote or by using ⌘-esc. Your desktop will disappear and Front Row's interface will fill the entire screen. Exit Front Row by depressing the esc key.

iCal

iCal is the built-in calender application in Snow Leopard. It has multiple view options, allows you to enter new events, set the duration of the event, and more. Since iCal talks to Mail, any To Dos you generate in iCal show up in your mailbox in the sidebar under Reminders. You can also publish (Calendar→Publish) and subscribe to other calendars, which is great for following your favorite team or keeping up with someone else's schedule. With iCal you aren't limited to one calendar; you can have as many as you like, so if you want to keep your work and personal calendars separate, you can.

iChat

iChat is a messaging system and a little more. You can have a text, audio, or video chat with another user (AIM and Jabber chat servers are supported as well), but you can do much more. You can show off your pictures with a slide show or give a keynote presentation over iChat. You can also set up conferences and have the participants chat with each other. iChat also offers the ability to share screens, which is a great way to troubleshoot a friend's or relative's Mac.

WARNING

If you're sharing your screen with another user, be aware that they can make changes, copy files, and delete things on your Mac just as you do when you're using it.

Snow Leopard has brought some improvements to iChat. Connections are now more stable and video chatting offers larger chat windows while using less bandwidth.

Image Capture

Image Capture lets your Mac transfer images from a camera or a scanner. This is useful if you have a bunch of images you need to download from a device into some place other than iPhoto, which can import images as well.

iSync

If you don't have an iPhone but do have a phone (or other device) that supports iSync, you can Sync the device with the contacts and calendars on your Mac. For a complete list of iSync supported devices, as well as links to drivers for some devices that are not supported out of the box, see *http://support .apple.com/kb/HT2824*.

NOTE

iSync no longer has anything to do with MobileMe (née .Mac). To sync computers and iPhones/iPod Touches with MobileMe, you'll have to head to the MobileMe Preference pane.

---

iTunes

iTunes started out life as a way to manage the music you ripped from your CD library. It is a lot more than that now. iTunes lets you buy music, buy TV shows, rent or buy movies, and, almost incidentally, manage your music, TV shows, podcasts, movies, and iPhone/iPod Touch App Store purchases.

Mail

Mail is the standard email client for Mac OS X. But there's more to Mail than just sending and receiving email. You can use Mail as your RSS reader, use Mail to store notes for yourself, and set up To Dos with an alarm. But that's not all. You can set up rules to handle incoming messages, sending them directly to a destination folder depending on the criteria you select (click Mail→Preferences and go to the Rules Preference pane).

For good or ill, you can also create fancy email with Mail by using stationery (Apple includes a number of templates). To access the templates, click the Stationery icon in the top of the New Message window. Your mail will be full of color (and likely annoyance) for all the readers of your missives. If you're looking for an easy method to attach photos (or to use them with Stationery), Mail includes a browser for all your photos stored in iPhoto. Click the Photo Browser icon and choose the picture you want to attach.

Mail also includes a search box in the upper-right of the toolbar. Finally you can set up Smart folders mailboxes in Mail to sort your mail for you. The following sections contain more information on using Mail.

Adding new accounts

When you first run Mail, it will offer to set up an email account for you. To add another account, select File→Add Account. In most cases, the only information you'll need to set up an account is your name, email address, and password. Type in those three bits of information and Mail will try to figure out how to configure your email server. If it can't, Mail will ask you to provide detailed settings, such as incoming server name, account type, and more. You can get that information from your administrator or Internet Service Provider.

Some email services, such as Google Mail, allow you to access your mail using either POP (Post Office Protocol) or IMAP (Internet Mail Access Protocol). If you like to access the same mail from multiple devices (such as an iPhone and/or another computer), IMAP is your best choice because all your mail is stored on the server; when you read a message, it is marked as read across all the devices you access it from. Some services may require you to enable IMAP before you can access them. To enable IMAP in a service such as Google Mail, log into your mail using a web browser, and visit Google Mail's settings to make sure that IMAP is enabled. You may also need to look on the mail service's settings screen (or in its help system) for instructions on configuring Mail to access it via IMAP.

Add a signature to outgoing mail

If you end all your mail with the same thing, all that typing is repetitive, even if it is only "Thanks, Chris." You can use a signature to automatically append a message or add a picture to the end of your messages.

To add a signature, go to Mail→Preferences (⌘-,), select the Signatures tab, and choose the account you want to add a signature to (or choose All Signatures to create a signature for all your accounts). Click the + button. Type the text you want to use in the third box in the window (Mail will automatically suggest your name and email). If you want to use an image (such as a picture of your actual signature) scan a picture of your signature, whittle it down to a small size (you can use Preview to change its size), and drag the image into the third box.

If you add more than one signature, you can click an option next to Choose Signature, which allows you to specify a signature or rotate through your signatures sequentially or randomly.

Enable junk mail filtering

Junk mail is almost universally reviled. Apple knows this, so Mail can automatically filter junk mail. Head to Mail→Preferences (⌘-,) and select the Junk Mail tab. Check the box next to Enable junk mail filtering to turn it on. You'll find choices to move the suspected junk mail to a Junk Mailbox or you can choose to leave it in your inbox. Note that every time you mark a message as junk, Mail will learn from this action and improve its junk mail filtering. Mail's junk mail filter isn't, of course, 100 percent accurate so if all your mail providers have their own server-side junk filtering, you may want to leave this disabled.

Manage mailboxes

To add a standard mailbox, click the + button found in the lower right corner of Mail and choose Add MailBox. You can add a Smart Mailbox from the same menu; you'll be presented with a window where you can set up search criteria for the new Smart Mailbox.

Quickly delete junk mail

If you've become confident in Mail's ability to figure out which mail is junk, you can get rid of it with Option-⌘-J or click to Mailbox→Erase Junk Mail.

Search your mail

You can use Spotlight to search for that elusive memo you want to reread, but if you use the search box found in Mail's menu bar, you won't have to wade through search results from other sources. You'll get the same lightning fast results, but you'll see only matches from your email, notes, and To Dos.

Photo Booth

Photo Booth is likely the silliest and most fun application included with Snow Leopard. With PhotoBooth, you can do something as simple as snapping a picture using the built-in iSight camera or something as complicated as filming a short movie with a fake background. Click the Effects button to choose all sorts of strange effects and backgrounds.

Preview

Preview is the default image viewer for the Mac. Any image you download in a common format such as *.jpg*, *.png*, or *.pdf* will be opened with Preview by default. You can resize, crop, and adjust colors in images, and annotate images and PDFs. You can also use Preview to snap screen shots, create icons, and more.

The version of Preview that ships with Snow Leopard offers a lot of improvements over the last version. Preview now features an annotation button, which places a toolbar at the bottom of the window so you can easily add comments and the like to the PDFs and images you are working with. You can also click Tools→Annotate to make changes.

Snow Leopard's Preview now supports scanning. Attach a scanner or an all-in-one printer to your Mac and you'll be able to scan an image directly in to Preview (File→Import from Scanner). And once you have that image (or any other) in Preview, you'll be able to scale it, crop it, or annotate it.

QuickTime Player

QuickTime is the technology behind much of Mac OS X's media savvy. Front Row, DVD Player, iTunes, and other applications rely heavily on QuickTime. QuickTime X is the new, improved version of QuickTime that comes with Snow Leopard.

The first thing you'll notice when you use the new version of QuickTime for watching a movie is nothing: all the buttons and sliders you are used to surrounding the file disappear while the movie is playing, you'll only see those when you slide the mouse over the movie.

There is more good news about QuickTime X. If you want to use QuickTime to watch a movie in full screen, you won't have to pony up the $29 for QuickTime Pro or resort to third-party tools. Most of the features of QuickTime Pro are now included in the standard edition of QuickTime X. You can perform simple trimming and record directly into QuickTime via your iSight, attached webcam, or microphone. Once you've created something you want to share with the world, you can post it directly from QuickTime to either YouTube, iTunes, or MobileMe using the Share drop-down menu found in QuickTime's menu bar.

There in one more killer feature found in QuickTime X: the ability to record your screen. Choose File→New Screen Recording, click the red circle, and you'll be off to the wonderful world of screencasting.

Safari

Safari is the slick web browser that comes with Mac OS X. It's built on the open source WebKit browser platform (*http://web kit.org*). Safari is both web standards-compliant and full-featured. There's a lot to Safari: the application does everything you expect a web browser to do and a little more, so getting Safari set up the way you want it to work is worth the effort.

Change the home page

When you get a new Mac, the default home page is *http://www .apple.com*. This is great if you love to keep up with Apple, but probably a bit boring for everyday use. To change the default home page go to Safari→Preferences (⌘-,) and select the General tab. Then type the URL of the web page you wish to use as your home page in the Home page text box.

Change the default browser

If you'd like to use another browser by default, such as Firefox, head to Safari→Preferences (⌘-,) and select the General tab. Next, choose the browser you want to use as your default browser from the pop-up menu labeled Default web browser.

Control which pages are shown in top sites

Safari 4 features a slick splash page, Top Sites (Shift-⌘-1), with snapshots of your most commonly visited sites. It's useful and visually appealing, but Safari might put some pages there that you don't want to see. You can edit the pages shown by clicking the Edit button in the lower lefthand corner. Pages you want to keep can be locked down with a pushpin, pages you don't want shown on the splash page can be banished by clicking the X. Finally, a blue star in the corner of a web page means that the page has been updated since your last visit.

You can add a bookmark directly to Top Sites by choosing Bookmark→Add Bookmark and specifying Top Sites as the location to store the bookmark. Top Sites bookmarks are not synced to MobileMe, so you should save the bookmark somewhere under your Bookmarks Bar or Bookmarks menu as well.

Find a page you didn't bookmark

It happens to everyone; you see an interesting site but you don't bother to bookmark it. Three days later, you want to find the site but you don't remember what is called or how you ended up at the site. Safari's history to the rescue. To bring up your history, select History→Show All History. Then type whatever snippet you remember about the mystery site in the search box (the one just below the Google search box). Safari returns all the web pages that contain what you're looking for.

Block pop-up ads

You probably find pop-up ads annoying. Turns out that Safari can block pop-ups. To enable pop-up blocking, click the Safari menu and click Block Pop-Up Windows (Shift-⌘-K). A checkmark next to that menu selection indicates the pop-up blocker is active.

Change where downloaded items are saved

By default, Safari saves downloaded items in the Downloads folder in your Home directory. You can get Safari to download to any location of your choosing. Click Safari→Preferences (⌘-,) and choose the General tab. Click Other from the Save downloaded files to pop-up menu, and choose where you want Safari to save downloads.

Control cookies

Most websites will send cookies (small bundles of data that are stored between sessions and visits to a website) to your browser. If you're concerned about how cookies are used, you can customize the way Safari handles them. Click Safari→Preferences (⌘-,) and go to the Security tab. Choose the setting you want in the Accept cookies. You can also examine all the cookies that Safari has by clicking Show cookies. From there, you can search, view, and remove cookies.

Get rid of Safari's history

You might find yourself on sites that you don't really want to be on. Then you might realize that the pages are stored in Safari's history. Although there are some things that once seen, cannot be unseen, you may still like to pretend that you never visited the site. If so, you can either delete Safari's entire history (History→Clear History) or delete any offending entries by hand (History→Show All History, select sites for deletion and hit the Delete key).

If you do nothing, Safari will still delete your browsing history after one month. If this interval is too long or too short for your tastes, you can change the amount of time Safari remembers what you've been looking at by adjusting Safari's preferences. Take a trip to Safari→Preferences, go to the General Preference pane, and adjust how long Safari saves your browsing habits with the pop-up menu next to Remove History Items. You can choose between one day and one year (at preset intervals) or take control of the situation and select manually.

Add a URL to the desktop

If you like to have the sites you frequently visit accessible directly from the desktop highlight the URL of the site you want on the desktop in Safari. Drag that directly to the desktop. You can also click and drag a site's *favicon* (the icon to the left of the page's address). The result will be a file icon (it will look like a piece of paper with a giant @ on it) with the URL or page title as the name. Now you can double-click this icon to load the page in your default browser. You can change the name of the icon by single-clicking the name and typing something more meaningful, just as you would with any other file.

Browse privately

There are times when you don't want Safari keeping track of your history; for those times, Private Browsing is the answer. To turn on Private Browsing, click Safari→Private Browsing. You'll be taken to a dialogue detailing just what Private Browsing does. Click OK to browse without having searches remembered in the search box, having sites you've visited added to Safari's history, or storing cookies permanently.

WARNING

Private Browsing isn't a "set it and forget it" option; it is good for your current session only. If you quit Safari, the next time you open Safari, Private Browsing will be inactive and Safari will diligently start recording all of your comings and goings on the Internet.

Make Safari remember passwords for website logins

This is a great time saver, although it is a bit of a security risk if you leave your Mac unattended while you're logged in (for a tip on making it a little safer, see "Password Management" on page 190). To get Safari to remember and automatically enter your login information for websites, click Safari→Preferences, choose AutoFill, and check the box next to Usernames and passwords. When you enter a username and password into a site, Safari will ask if you want to save it.

You may find that some sites, especially banking and credit card sites, do not allow their passwords to be saved.

Use a different default RSS reader

Safari is the default RSS reader in Mac OS X. But you might like to use Mail or a third-party RSS reader such as NetNews-Wire. To make this change, select Safari→Preferences (⌘-,). Click the RSS tab and select the RSS reader of your choice from the pop-up menu next to Default RSS reader.

Customize Safari's toolbar

Safari's default toolbar is missing some buttons you might want, such as the Home button, which takes you to your home page. You can add buttons to Safari's toolbar by going to View→Customize Toolbar and dragging the buttons you want on to Safari's toolbar. To get rid of the things you don't want on Safari's toolbar, you can right-click or Control-click on the offending item and choose Remove Item.

Stickies

Stickies are a virtual version of Post-it® notes. Fire up this application and you can leave notes all over your desktop. Select File→New or press ⌘-N, and you'll end up with a blank note you can type into, add images to, and use for reminders. When that quick list on a sticky becomes something you need to share, you can export your sticky note as rich text (File→Export Text).

System Preferences

System Preferences is the place to tweak Mac OS X. System Preferences are covered more completely in Chapter 5.

TextEdit

What could an application with a name like TextEdit possibly do? That's right, TextEdit is a not-too-shabby word processor (although earlier versions of it were limited, it keeps getting new features with every new version of Mac OS X). If you use TextEdit, you can write the great American novel or a grocery list. Snow Leopard's system-wide spell checker is available, and you can also add a grammar check (select TextEdit→Preferences, then click Check grammar with spelling). TextEdit's default format for saving files is *.rtf* (Rich Text Format), but you can also save (and open) in HTML, OpenOffice.org (*.odt*) or Microsoft Word 97, 2003, or 2007.

NOTE

You can even add text styles in TextEdit. Select some text and use the Format menu to format it the way you want it. Then, with the text still selected, click the Styles menu at the top of the editing window, choose Other, then click Add to Favorites. You'll be able to give the file a name for future use.

Time Machine

You know you *should* back up your computer, and you know you *need* to back up your computer. The problem is that it is such a hassle. The hassle factor is gone with Time Machine. Time Machine automates the backing up process and puts a beautiful front graphical user interface on flipping back in time. To use Time Machine, all you really need is an attached drive with sufficient space. You can also use another Mac as a backup

---

target or Apple's Time Capsule to back up your Mac over the network.

NOTE

You might assume you could plug a hard drive into an Airport Base Station and use Time Machine on that disk. Your choices are limited to another Mac, a Time Capsule, or an attached drive.

Time Capsule operates seamlessly once it is set up and turned on. To set it up, connect a suitable drive, and when asked, confirm that you want to use it as a Time Machine disk. After it's up and running, you can make a few adjustments. When you launch Time Machine (System Preferences→Time Machine), you'll notice a big sliding On/Off button, a button to bring up the Select Disk dialogue, and an Options button. The Options button lets you specify which folders and drives you don't want backed up. Just click the + button and select the items you want to exclude.

Using Time Machine is intuitive when you're looking for a file you accidentally deleted (click the Time Machine menu extra and enter Time Machine, then navigate through the available backups). But if you want to restore your system from a Time Machine backup, you'll need to first boot from a Mac OS X install disk. Once you have booted up and have picked your installation language, don't start the installation of Mac OS X. Instead, click the menu bar and select Utilities. The last option in the drop-down menu is Restore System From Backup. Selecting that option will allow you to select the Time Machine disk or Time Capsule you want to use to restore your system.

Utilities Included with Snow Leopard

What is the difference between an application and a utility? It is largely semantic. You can argue that, in general, applications allow you to create and modify data while utilities allow you to monitor and manage your Mac. To be certain, utilities are applications, just usually not as exciting as the applications you'll find in the rest of the Applications folder (there is a reason Utilities is a subfolder of Applications and not the other way around).

That doesn't mean that the Utilities folder is full of arcane and very boring stuff. There are plenty of useful applications inside. You'll imagine great uses for a lot of the utilities installed with Snow Leopard once you get a quick peek at what they do.

Activity Monitor

The main window of Activity Monitor gives you a sortable list (click on the column heading) of all the processes running on your Mac. You can view stats about CPU load, System Memory, Disk Activity, Disk Usage, or your Network. Clicking on a single process, then clicking on the Inspect icon allows a close look at the process. You can also use Activity Monitor to quit any process by selecting the process and clicking the Quit icon (very useful when a program is needlessly hogging the processor or unresponsive).

NOTE

Activity Monitor displays a constantly running graph of system usage in the Dock. You can control what data is being displayed by right-clicking on the Dock icon and choosing the data you want Disk Utility to display in the Dock.

Airport Utility

If you own a Time Capsule, an Airport Base Station, or an Airport Express, use this utility to manage those devices.

AppleScript Editor

AppleScript is a programming language that is designed to be easy to use. AppleScript can control scriptable applications on your Mac (most, but not all, applications) allowing you to generate scripts that can, for example, resize photos automatically. AppleScript is capable of much more and using the AppleScript Editor allows you to write, edit, test, run, and compile Apple-Scripts. For more information, see *http://developer.apple.com/applescript/*.

Audio MIDI Setup

MIDI is an acronym for Musical Instrument Digital Interface. With that in mind, you can probably guess that Audio MIDI Setup is used to hook musical instruments to your computer. This is useful for fans of GarageBand who want to hook up MIDI instruments to their Mac.

Bluetooth File Exchange

Use this utility to send files to supported Bluetooth devices, such as phones, PDAs, or other computers. Bluetooth is slower than Wi-Fi but requires less setup to transfer files. After you run this utility, you can either drag the file you want to transfer onto the Bluetooth Dock icon and wait for a list of recipients to appear, or select a file in the Bluetooth File Exchange window and hit the Send button (where again you'll have to wait for the list of possible recipients to appear).

Boot Camp Assistant

The Boot Camp Assistant will let you install Windows (XP, Vista, or later) on any Mac running Snow Leopard. The assistant will partition your hard drive and install the necessary drivers. You'll be required to supply a Windows installation disk. Once installed, you'll have a dual boot Mac capable of running Snow Leopard or Windows. You choose which operating system to boot into using the Start Up Disk Preference pane.

NOTE

Boot Camp isn't the only way to get Windows on your Mac. There are several third-party programs that will let you run Windows and Snow Leopard at the same time, as opposed to Boot Camp, which requires you to reboot the computer when you want to switch operating systems. Two popular ones are Parallels Desktop and VMware Fusion.

ColorSync Utility

Because everyone sees colors a little differently, and because devices often interpret colors in different ways, ColorSync is included in Mac OS X to manage colors. ColorSync Utility allows you to repair ICC (International Color Consortium) profiles on your Mac (click the First Aid icon). ColorSync also allows you to inspect the profiles used by your Mac, displaying a groovy 3-D plot of the profile when you click the Profiles icon. The Devices icon lets you manage the ColorSync profiles of attached devices. ColorSync Utility also allows you to apply filters to, for example, a PDF document with the Filters icon. Finally, the Calculator icon allows you to sample any pixel displayed on your computer and find the values for it (click the magnifying glass icon on this page).

Console

Unlike your car keys, your Mac keeps track of itself. Every time something unexpected (or even routine) happens, the system notes the problem and posts it in a log. However, the logs are a bit difficult to find. This is where Console comes in. With Console, you can review the errors logged on your Mac much more conveniently than if you had to dig through the Library folder. Clicking on the Show Log List icon lets you see all the logs available on your computer. The logs contain information critical for diagnosing bugs you send to Apple and can be useful in tracking a problematic application.

NOTE

If you open Console, you'll see a lot of messages. There isn't any reason to worry, as Mac OS X logs a lot of information. You can use the search box or click on a specific log in the Log List to filter out the unwanted information.

Digital Color Meter

With this utility you can inspect the color values of anything displayed on screen. Set the size of the aperture (all the way down to a single pixel), and choose from a multitude of ways the results can be calculated, ranging from RGB to Tristimulus.

Disk Utility

Disk Utility is a toolbox for all your disks. You can use Disk Utility to erase disks (including CD-RW and DVD-RW), format disks, mount and unmount disks (if you've ejected an attached disk, you can remount it without unplugging/replugging it using Disk Utility's mount icon), format disks, securely delete data, create compressed or uncompressed disk images, repair permissions, format disks, partition disks, and more. For information on using Disk Utility to check your drive's health, see "Startup Problems" on page 107.

Exposé

Double clicking the Exposé icon invokes Exposé. Exposé is covered in more detail in "Exposé" on page 94.

Grab

Grab is Mac OS X's built-in screen capture utility. With Grab you can capture a section of the screen, a complete window (sans the drop shadow), the entire screen, or a timed screen. The timed screen option gives you 10 seconds to get whatever process you're trying to capture running. All the images are saved in *.tiff* format.

Grapher

Grapher is a program that displays graphs of equations that are built-in to the program, as well as equations you enter. Grapher can handle a wide range of coordinate (polar, cylindrical, cartesian, and spherical) choices, and will even generate 3-D graphs. This is a useful tool for someone studying calculus.

Java Preferences

No, the question isn't about with milk or without; the question is what you want the Java programming language to do for you and how. If you use Java-based applications often, this utility allows you to select your preferred version, manage security, and configure debugging.

Keychain Access

Keychain Access stores your passwords for the moments when you inevitably forget them. As long as you remember your system password, you can recover any password stored in the Keychain (many third-party programs, like Firefox, do not use Keychain). You can also create secure notes readable only in Keychain that are locked with your password. For more information on Keychain Access, see Chapter 8.

Migration Assistant

When you first set up your Mac, you had the option of transferring your data from another computer. You were also assured that if you didn't want to transfer your data right then, you could do it later. For more information on all the ways you can transfer data using Migration Assistant, see "Moving Data and Applications from Another Mac" on page 23.

Network Utility

Network Utility offers an interface for common networking tasks. Most users will find the Info button of the most immediate use. For those familiar with Unix network diagnostics, there are also buttons for Netstat, Ping, Lookup, Traceroute, Whois, Finger, and Port Scan.

Podcast Capture

If you don't have access to a Mac running Mac OS X Server (Leopard or later), this tool is useless to you. If you do have access, Podcast Capture lets you produce and distribute podcasts with ease.

RAID Utility

Got a RAID card installed in your Mac? No? Then forget this utility. If you do have a RAID (Redundant Array of Inexpensive

Disks) card (only available for Mac Pros and Xserves at a cost of $700 as of this writing), RAID Utility will allow you to configure a RAID array on your system.

Remote Install Mac OS X

This utility allows you to install Snow Leopard on a Mac without a DVD drive. Currently the only Mac shipping that lacks a DVD drive is the MacBook Air. If you own a MacBook Air and are upgrading to Snow Leopard, fire this up and follow the directions.

System Profiler

System Profiler will tell you just about everything you want to know about your Mac. Hardware, networks, and software are all covered in great detail. If you're wondering about any particular aspect of your Mac, System Profiler is the place to look.

NOTE

You can also invoke System Profiler by clicking the Apple menu, choosing About This Mac, and clicking the More Info button.

Terminal

Mac OS X is built on Unix. The Terminal application is your window into this world. Unix is incredibly powerful and you can run Unix commands from the Terminal. Clicking Help→Terminal Help will get you started if you aren't familiar with it. The most important Terminal tip? When you're confused, typing **man** *command-name* brings up a manual page where you can learn about a particular Unix command (try **man man** for starters).

VoiceOver

VoiceOver is Mac OS X's screen reading software. It describes what is happening on your screen using one of the voices installed with OS X. This utility allows you to customize VoiceOver's settings. With this utility you can control what voice is used, how your computer is navigated when using VoiceOver, how VoiceOver handles web pages, how the keys on the keyboard control your Mac, and set up a braille monitor. For additional information, see "Seeing tab" on page 153.

X11

X11 is the Mac OS X version of the X Window System, which allows your Mac to run many graphical Unix applications.

CHAPTER 7

MobileMe

There's a good chance that you have more than one device connected to the Internet. You might have two Macs, a Mac and a PC, a Mac and an iPhone, or any combination of devices mentioned (plus others). All those devices have a lot of data on them. You have settings, bookmarks, contacts, and more. MobileMe makes the chore of keeping your devices in sync less onerous by taking most of the work out of it for you.

MobileMe is the successor to .Mac, but it hasn't changed a whole lot. MobileMe is a paid subscription service that gives you some storage space on servers run by Apple (20 GB, although this may change in future) for a personal account that includes email, file storage, and website hosting (there are limits on the monthly data transfer). MobileMe also offers the ability to keep your computers (Macs and, to some extent, Windows-based machines) synced with each other. For a free trial, go to *http://www.apple.com/mobileme/* or head to the MobileMe preference pane in System Preferences.

Using MobileMe with your Mac is easy; everything is built right in. But chances are that you don't exclusively use a Mac, so you'll want to use MobileMe on your Windows-based machine as well, since you've got data you want updated on your Windows machine too, right? You have to go to *http://www.apple .com/mobileme/features/pc.html* to get MobileMe working on your Windows-based machine. You'll need to have iTunes installed, then you'll need to install the MobileMe control panel. Once you've installed the control panel, you'll be able to sync Outlook, Outlook Express, and Windows contacts if you are using XP or Vista.

NOTE

You won't be able to sync Outlook if Outlook is using Microsoft Exchange Server. But Apple's Mail, Address Book, and Calendar can connect to Exchange Servers. To add an Exchange server, open iCal, choose iCal→Preferences, and click the Accounts icon at the top of the Preferences window. Press the + button to add your Exchange account (you'll need to get the settings from your Exchange administrator).

With MobileMe, you can sync the following (third-party applications may install other MobileMe sync options):

- Bookmarks
- Calendars
- Contacts
- Dashboard widgets
- Dock items
- Keychains
- Mail accounts
- Mail rules, signatures, and smart mailboxes
- Notes
- Preferences

Once MobileMe is set up, you'll not only have a cool *me.com* email address, but you'll have a place to host videos, pictures, and websites on the Internet. You'll also be able to (if you have more than one Mac) use Back to My Mac.

Back to My Mac

Back to My Mac is a killer feature of MobileMe that allows you to access your Mac from another Mac, as long as both of them are connected to the Internet. Back to My Mac pulls this trick off by using *wide area Bonjour* to automatically configure services over the Internet. To access your Mac, the user has to know your password, and the Mac has to be registered to the same account on MobileMe. Data transferred between computers is encrypted.

The weakest link in the Back to My Mac security scheme is likely your MobileMe password. If someone can guess that, you'd be in for some trouble. The best idea, and one recommended by Apple, is to make a strong password for your MobileMe account. For tips on making a great password, see "Password Management" on page 190.

To turn on Back to My Mac, go to System Preferences→MobileMe, select the Back to My Mac tab, and click Start. You'll also have to head to Sharing Preferences to turn on the specific sharing options you want available. You'll find a convenient button called Open Sharing Preferences in the Back to My Mac tab. You'll have to do this on each Mac you want to access remotely. As long as you are using the Sharing preference pane, you should take a moment to restrict who can access your Mac. Clicking the radio button to restrict access to Only these users and adjusting those users with the + and – buttons is an extra level of security that Apple recommends MobileMe users take.

Once Back to My Mac is enabled, you'll be interested in how it works. Accessible Macs will show up in the sidebar of a Finder window under the SHARED entry. Click the entry for the Mac you want to use and a window will open with buttons to Share Screen or Connect As options. Choosing Connect As will open a dialogue box where you'll need to type your username and password. Once you are connected, you'll be able to browse the computer with all the privileges you would have if you were sitting in front of the machine. You'll be able to copy files to and from the Mac you're connected to, move files around on the connected Mac, and even delete files.

If you choose Share Screen, you'll get the same log in dialogue, but once you're logged in, you'll be looking at the remote Mac's screen in a window on your computer as shown in Figure 7-1.

Figure 7-1. Your Mac in a window

With screen sharing, you'll get total control over the remote Mac. You can run applications, copy files, install applications, and even browse the Web with the remote Mac. The experience isn't as snappy as using the Mac that's right in front of you, and will depend on the connection speed of both computers. However, Back to My Mac can be a real lifesaver when you've left that important document at home.

Adding or Removing a Computer to/from MobileMe

To register or unregister a computer, go to System Preferences, and choose MobileMe→Sync→Advanced. From there you can click Register Computer to register the computer you're currently using. You can also remove any computers you don't want accessing your MobileMe account by clicking on the computer's name and clicking the Stop Syncing Computer button.

iDisk

There are a lot of ways to mount your iDisk. You can choose it from the sidebar of a Finder window, use the Go menu in the Finder (Go→iDisk→My iDisk), or use a key combination (Shift-⌘-I).

For information on checking free space, configuring iDisk syncing, or allowing others to access your iDisk, see "iDisk tab" on page 141.

Clearing the MobileMe Sync Slate

With MobileMe, you can choose what to sync and what not to sync between computers. You might want to sync bookmarks on one computer, but not Mail rules. If you decide at a later date to start syncing something you haven't synced in a long time, you may find that the discrepancy between machines has gotten so big that you get a lot of errors when you try to sync. One way to deal with this is to wipe the slate clean and do a full sync for all the machines.

If you have one computer with all the information you want to keep, you can force MobileMe to use that data. Pilot your Mac to System Preferences→MobileMe→Sync, then click Advanced and click Reset Sync Data. Next to "Replace," you'll find a drop-down menu that will allow you to specify what data you want to replace (All Sync Info or a specific set of data) and a cool animated arrow showing whether you'll be replacing the information on your computer or on MobileMe. Click the arrow under the cloud icon to replace all the data on MobileMe with data from the computer. Click Replace and the data on MobileMe will be overwritten.

Perform a sync and then you'll be ready to bring your other computers in line with the first computer. Follow the same steps just described, but instead of replacing data on MobileMe, replace the data on each of the computers you wish to sync, as shown in Figure 7-2.

Figure 7-2. Replacing the data on MobileMe

CHAPTER 8

Security

When you first boot that new Mac and set up a user, the system is configured to automatically log in. That is probably fine if you're the only person using your Mac, but not so great if your Mac is sitting out where a lot of people have access to it. Customize your security (log in and log out options) to fit the environment where you'll be using your Mac. If it is a desktop machine and you'll only be using it at home, you probably don't have much to worry about. If it is a MacBook that you plan on hauling everywhere you go, you'll want a little more security.

NOTE

See "Logging In" on page 40 to find out how to disable automatic login.

Security with Mac OS X usually comes down to passwords. Passwords for services, passwords for your account, passwords for websites, passwords for email. Once you have your Mac secured in a comfortable fashion, you will want to turn your attention to managing all those pesky but necessary passwords.

Password Management

The more you do online, the more you need passwords. Ideally, you want different passwords for everything; having your bank account password be the same password you use to post to a third-rate message board isn't the best idea. However, with so many passwords running around, it is easy to forget them. We've all been faced with the situation where we were sure we typed in the right password only to be repeatedly denied access. Fortunately, Mac OS X can help.

Recovering a Forgotten Password

So you've forgotten a password to some rarely visited yet essential server or some network you only join rarely. Turns out Snow Leopard probably has remembered the password for you (to have it save passwords for websites, see "Make Safari remember passwords for website logins" on page 171). To recover the password, open Keychain Access (*/Applications/ Utilities/Keychain Access*) and type the name of the site, application, or something relevant into the search box of Keychain Access. Double-click that item and a window will pop up with a checkbox to display the password. Check the box, enter your Mac OS X password when prompted, and you'll see a readable password.

NOTE

For an added level of security, you can configure Mac OS X to lock your keychain after a period of inactivity. Open Keychain Access (located in */Applications/Utilities*), click on your Login keychain, and select Edit→Change settings for keychain "login." You'll be able to lock the keychain after a period of inactivity or lock it when the computer sleeps. When you visit a website that needs to use a saved password, you'll have to type your login password to unlock your keychain.

Make a Great Password

The following passwords are not acceptable: letmein, password, 123, and qwerty. Using one of those for anything you care about is like leaving the door to your house wide open, but picking up the welcome mat. Sure, a miscreant might pause momentarily when they notice that the welcome mat is missing, but that won't stop them from coming in your house. You need a better password.

Just what makes a password good? You can find out if your chosen password is strong with Keychain Access; you can test out the strength of your password with its Password Assistant. You can't access Password Assistant directly, so you'll have to use Keychain Access (actually any prompt that displays the little key symbol will give you access to Password Assistant, but Keychain Access is one of the easiest ways to get there). Open Keychain Access (*/Applications/Utilities/Keychain Access*), then select Edit→Change Password for *some keychain*. You're not interested in changing the password for that keychain, what you're after is the Password Assistant (so just click Cancel when you are done experimenting).

NOTE

There is an excellent free utility that will invoke Password Assistant any time you want to generate a password. To get a copy, point your browser to *http://www .codepoetry.net/products/passwordassistant* and grab a copy of the time-saving application.

After you click the key symbol, a window will pop up that can rate your password (Figure 8-1). If your password isn't the digital equivalent of Fort Knox, try out some new passwords to see how they rate. If you can't come up with a good one on your own, Snow Leopard is happy to pitch in and help. It can suggest a "memorable" password or a password with letters and numbers, numbers only, a random password, or a

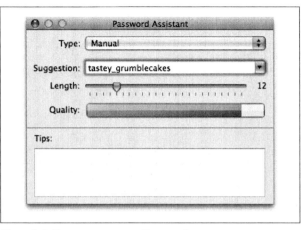

Figure 8-1. Know your password's strength

FIPS-181 (Federal Information Processing Standards publication 181) compliant password.

Storing Secure Notes

Keychain is great at storing passwords, but you can also use it to store notes. To write a note that no one else can see (well, except someone who has your username and password), open Keychain Access (*/Applications/Utilities/Keychain Access*), click the "login" keychain, select Secure Notes from the category section, and hit the + button found at the bottom of the window. Give your secret note a title and start typing away. When you're done, click Add and your note will be safely stored in the Keychain, as shown in Figure 8-2.

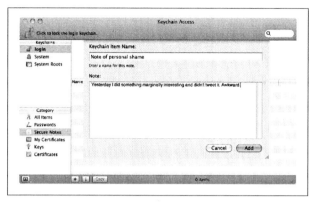

Figure 8-2. They must never know

Add a Keychain Access Menu Extra to the Menu Bar

With all the goodness associated with the Keychain, you might
want easy access to it. You can add it your dock, but that might
be getting a little crowded, and the Keychain icon isn't the best
looking icon Apple has churned out. Luckily, you can add a
menu extra for Keychain Access. The next time you're using
Keychain Access, go to Preferences (⌘-,) and in the General
tab, check the box next to Show Status in menu bar.

CHAPTER 9

Keyboard Commands and Special Characters

When you're using the keyboard, you want to keep your hands on the keyboard. A trip to the mouse or a hunt for a special character can really slow you down. The good news is that Snow Leopard has both a great many key commands and a great many special characters built-in. The bad news is that unless you're one of those people who remember the digits of Pi to a thousand places for fun, you won't remember them all.

The most important key commands and special characters vary from user to user. For example, if you're writing about Exposé, knowing how to type é really helps, but knowing how to type ¬ isn't of much use. Everyone uses their Mac a little differently, so this chapter features a large selection of keyboard commands and ways to type different characters. Pick the ones you'll use, remember them, and you'll save a lot of time and effort.

Key Commands

Imagine you're working on the next great novel. You've just written the key opening sentence of a paragraph that will re-define literature for centuries to come and you naturally want to save the document for posterity. You reach for the mouse, slide it up to the menu bar and select Save from the application menu. Your document is committed to the hard drive but your train of thought has been interrupted; what could have been the seminal paragraph of literature is now just a nifty opening sentence.

That example is extreme but illustrative—the less time you mouse, the more you produce when you're using the keyboard. While you'll want to learn the keyboard commands for all your favorite programs, some commands are so common that reserving a special spot for them in (your) memory is worthwhile:

⌘-S

Save. This saves the document you're working on. The more often you use ⌘-S, the happier you'll be. Nothing is more frustrating than having all your hard work disappear when the power flickers or an application crashes.

⌘-C

Copy. This command copies the current selection for later pasting.

⌘-V

Paste. Once you've copied something, you'll want to paste it.

⌘-X

Cut. This command deletes the current selection. After you've cut something, you can paste it elsewhere until you copy or cut something else.

⌘-,

Opens the preferences for the active application.

⌘-[and ⌘-]

Moves forward (+) and backwards (–) in the Finder, Safari, and some other applications.

⌘-?

Opens the Help dialogue for quick answers to your vexing questions.

⌘-Q

> Quits the current application. You can't easily quit the Finder, so this command doesn't work when you are using it. To quit the Finder (well, to relaunch it), see "The finder stops responding" on page 102.

⌘-Tab

> When you use this key command, you bring up the application switcher. Cycle through running applications by pressing Tab as you hold down ⌘. When you get to the application you are after, let go. If your hands are on the keyboard, this in a much faster way to switch applications than the Dock.

Option-⌘-esc

> Force quits the current program.

NOTE

If you're using a keyboard designed for Windows systems, you won't see the ⌘ key. Use the Windows key, which is usually in the same location you'd find the ⌘ key. Some keyboards use a different symbol (for example, the Happy Hacking Keyboard uses the "lozenge" symbol, ◊).

Once you've mastered those commands, your appetite for keyboard shortcuts is likely to become insatiable. Fortunately, there are plenty more of that keyboard shortcut, time saving goodness, many of which are shown in Table 9-1.

WARNING

Unfortunately, some of these commands are not supported uniformly across all programs. For example, in the Finder and many other applications, ⌘-I displays an informational dialogue (Get Info) for the currently selected file or object, but in most word processing applications, ⌘-I italicizes the selected text.

On some keyboards, you may need to hold down the key labeled Fn to use keyboard shortcuts that require a function key (F1, F2, etc.).

Table 9-1. Common keyboard shortcuts

Key command	Most common action	Finder action
⌘-A	Selects all	Selects all items in current directory
⌘-B	Makes selected text bold (in word processing programs).	None
⌘-C	Copies selection	Copies selected files and folders
⌘-D	Duplicates selected object (usually in drawing applications)	Duplicates selected file or folder
⌘-E	Searches for highlighted text	Ejects disk
⌘-F	Finds text	Opens a new Finder window with cursor in search field
⌘-H	Hides current application	Hides Finder
⌘-I	Italicizes selected text.	Opens Get Info window on selected item
⌘-J	Jumps to currently selected text (useful if you've selected some text, then scrolled elsewhere in a document)	Shows View options
⌘-K	Clears screen (Terminal); inserts hyperlink (text editors, word processors, and Mail)	Opens Connect to Server window
⌘-L	Goes to line number (common in text editors)	Creates Alias
⌘-M	Minimizes window	Same
⌘-N	Creates new document	New Finder window

Key command	Most common action	Finder action
⌘-O	Displays Open File dialogue	Opens selected item
⌘-P	Prints	None
⌘-Q	Quits current application	None
⌘-R	Varies	Shows original file when an alias is selected
⌘-S	Saves current file	None
⌘-T	Displays Font panel	Adds selected item to Finder window sidebar
⌘-V	Pastes copied item	Pastes copied file(s) or folder(s)
⌘-W	Closes window	Same
⌘-X	Cuts	None
⌘-Z	Undoes most recent action	Same
⌘-1	Varies	View Finder items as icons
⌘-2	Varies	View Finder items as list
⌘-3	Varies	View Finder items as columns
⌘-4	Varies	View Finder items in Cover Flow View
⌘-esc	Activates Front Row	Same
⌘-Delete	Varies	Moves selected item to Trash
⌘-Tab	Opens Application Switcher	Same
⌘-[	Goes back (when using web browsers)	Goes back one directory
⌘-]	Goes forward (when using web browsers)	Goes forward one directory
⌘-?	Activates Help menu	Same

Key command	Most common action	Finder action
⌘-Space	Activates Spotlight search	Same
⌘-`	Cycles through application windows	Cycles through Finder windows
Tab	Moves focus to next item or inserts tab (in text editors)	Moves focus to next item
Shift-⌘-3	Takes a picture of the screen; saves image file to desktop	Same
Shift-⌘-4	Displays a cursor for taking a snapshot of part of the screen. Press space to take a picture of a single window; saves image file to desktop	Same
Shift-Control-⌘-3	Works as ⌘-Shift-3, but copies picture to clipboard	Same
Shift-Control-⌘-4	Works as ⌘-Shift-4, but copies picture to clipboard	Same
Shift-⌘-A	Varies	Opens Applications folder
Shift-⌘-C	Varies	Opens Computer folder
Shift-⌘-D	Varies	Opens Desktop folder
Shift-⌘-O	Varies	Opens Documents folder
Shift-⌘-G	Varies	Opens Go to folder dialogue box
Shift-⌘-H	Varies	Opens Home folder
Shift-⌘-I	Varies	Opens iDisk
Shift-⌘-K	Varies	Opens Network folder
Shift-⌘-N	Varies	Creates a new folder
Shift-⌘-Q	Displays logout dialogue, will log out automatically after one minute	Same
Shift-⌘-S	Opens Save As... dialogue	None

Key command	Most common action	Finder action
Shift-⌘-U	Varies	Opens Utilities folder
Shift-⌘-Delete	Varies	Opens Empty Trash dialogue
Shift-Option-⌘-Delete	Varies	Empties Trash immediately
Option (while dragging)	Copies item to new location	Copies file/folder to new location
⌘-Option (while dragging)	Varies	Creates an alias to a file/folder at new location
Option-⌘-D	Shows or hides Dock	Same
Option-⌘-M	Varies	Minimizes all windows
Option-⌘-esc	Forces an application to quit	Same
Option-⌘-Eject	Puts computer to sleep	Same
Control-Eject	Shows the Restart, Sleep, Shutdown dialogue box	Same
Control-⌘-Eject	Quits all applications and restart	Same
Control-F2 (Control-Fn-F2 on notebook Macs)	Moves keyboard focus to the menu	Same
Control-F3 (Control-Fn-F3 on notebook Macs)	Moves keyboard focus to the Dock	Same
Control-F4 (Control-Fn-F4 on notebook Macs)	Moves focus to active window or cycles through windows	Same
Control-F5 (Control-Fn-F5 on notebook Macs)	Moves keyboard focus to the window's toolbar	Same
Control-F6 (Control-Fn-F6 on notebook Macs)	Moves focus to the floating window, such as the Formatting Palette in Microsoft Office	Same
Control-F7 (Control-Fn-F7 on notebook Macs)	Toggles behavior of the Tab key (Tab moves between text boxes and lists or between all controls)	Same

Key command	Most common action	Finder action
Control-F8 (Control-Fn-F8 on notebook Macs)	Moves keyboard focus to menu extra region in the menu bar	Same

You're probably not going to remember all of those keyboard shortcuts but you likely will remember the ones you use frequently, and more time at the keyboard means less time wasted mousing and searching for commands.

Customizing Key Commands

If you don't like the key commands built into Mac OS X, you don't have to put up with them. You can change the key commands or add your own by taking a trip to the Keyboard Preference pane. For more information, see "Keyboard shortcuts" on page 133.

Typing Special Characters in Mac OS X

If you're banging away on the keyboard and find yourself wanting to type special characters (say the é in Exposé, for example) and using convoluted methods to get the character you want (pasting them from the Web, and so on) you might be wondering if there is a mouseless way to do it. Don't fret, you don't have to go through life searching for an easy way to type é. Table 9-2 shows how to type this and other diacritic symbols.

Table 9-2. Diacritic accent mark shortcuts

Symbol	Name	Keystroke
´	Acute	Option-E, then type the letter
^	Circumflex	Option-I, then type the letter
`	Grave	Option-`, then type the letter
˜	Tilde	Option-N, then type the letter
¨	Umlaut	Option-U, then type the letter

That takes care of only a few characters you may not be able to find on your keyboard. But what about other characters, such as the Euro symbol or the Apple logo? You might try looking through the Font Book utility, but there are so many fonts installed on a Mac that you will likely never find what you want. However, the Character Palette is a bit easier to use: you can enable it by heading to System Preferences, and selecting Language & Text. Next, select the Input Sources tab, and check the box labeled Keyboard & Character Viewer. You'll get a new icon on the menu bar that lets you launch either the Character Viewer or the Keyboard Viewer. Character Viewer lets you browse a wide variety of special characters and insert them into a document with the Insert button. With Keyboard Viewer up, as shown in Figure 9-1, you can hold down the Shift, Option, or Shift-Option keys to see how the keyboard is modified when you're depressing the modifier keys.

Figure 9-1. Wonder what the Option key does to the characters on your keyboard? Wonder no more!

You can also check out Table 9-3 for a quick reference to U.S. English keyboard modifiers.

Table 9-3. Special character shortcuts on a U.S. English keyboard

No modifiers	Shift	Option	Shift-Option
`	~	` (above next vowel typed)	`
1	!	¡	(fraction slash symbol)
2	@	™	€
3	#	£	‹
4	$	¢	›
5	%	∞	fi (ligature)
6	^	§	fl (ligature)
7	&	¶	‡
8	*	•	°
9	(	ª	·
0	)	º	‚
-	_	–	—
=	+	≠	±
q	Q	œ	Œ
w	W	∑	„
e	E	´ (above next vowel typed)	´
r	R	®	‰
t	T	†	ˇ
y	Y	¥	Á
u	U	¨ (above next vowel typed)	¨
i	I	ˆ (above next vowel typed)	ˆ
o	O	ø	Ø
p	P	π	∏
[	{	"	"
]	}	'	'
\	|	«	»
a	A	å	Å
s	S	ß	∫

No modifiers	Shift	Option	Shift-Option
d	D	∂	Î
f	F	ƒ	Ï
g	G	©	˝
h	H	˙	Ó
j	J	Δ	Ô
k	K	˚	(Apple logo)
l	L	¬	Ò
;	:	…	Ú
'	"	æ	Æ
z	Z	Ω	¸
x	X	≈	˛
c	C	ç	Ç
v	V	√	◊
b	B	∫	ı
n	N	~ (above next "n" typed)	˜
m	M	µ	Â
,	<	≤	¯
.	>	≥	˘
/	?	÷	¿

Index

Symbols

^ symbolizing Control key,
ix
⌘ key, ix, 197

A

About Application Name, 46
About this Mac menu, 43
accounts (see user accounts)
Accounts menu, 52
Accounts Preference pane,
145
Activity Monitor, 175
Additional Fonts option, 21
Address Book, 158
Administrator account, 32
Advanced preferences
(Finder), 61
Airport utility, 175
alert sounds, 138
aliasing files and folders, 65

Appearance preference pane,
118
Apple applications and
utilities, migrating from
another Mac, 25
Apple Events, 145
Apple ID, 23
Apple menu for Snow
Leopard, 43
Apple Remote Desktop, 144
AppleJack, 113
AppleScript Editor, 176
Application menu, 46
listing of typical items, 46
Services, 48
standard Application
menus, 48
Application Switcher, 78
applications
64-bit, 3
enhancements under Snow
Leopard, 8
iChat, 8

We'd like to hear your suggestions for improving our indexes. Send email to
index@oreilly.com.

Preview, 9
QuickTime X, 10
installed with Snow
        Leopard, 158–174
    Address Book, 158
    Automator, 159
    Calculator, 159
    Chess, 160
    Dashboard, 160
    DVD Player, 161
    Font Book, 162
    Front Row, 162
    iCal, 162
    iChat, 163
    Image Capture, 163
    iSync, 163
    iTunes, 164
    Mail, 164
    Photo Booth, 167
    Preview, 167
    QuickTime X, 167
    Safari, 168
    Stickies, 172
    System Preferences,
        173
    TextEdit, 173
    Time Machine, 174
migrating from another
        Mac, 24
misbehaving, 100
PowerPC, running on
        Snow Leopard, 6
Archive and Install option,
    18
Audio MIDI Setup, 176
Automatic View (Stack), 74
Automator, 159

B

Back to My Mac (MobileMe),
    185
backing up the hard drive, 18
backups using Time Machine,
    174
    migrating data from, 27
battery problems,
        troubleshooting, 104
Battery tab (Energy Saver
        Preference pane), 130
Bluetooth File Exchange, 176
Bluetooth keyboard, setting
        up, 134
Bluetooth Sharing option,
    145
Boot Camp Assistant, 177
booting failure,
        troubleshooting, 110
booting Mac OS X
    from another disk, 112
    in single user mode, using
        AppleJack, 113
Burn button for Finder
        toolbar, 58
Burn folders, 82

C

Calculator, 159
calendar application (iCal),
    162
CDs
    CDs and DVDs Preference
        pane, 129
    duplicating, 68
    sharing, 142
Character Palette, 203

chatting
    iChat application, 163
    Parental Controls on, 149
Chess, 160
chips
    64-bit, 3
    multiple processing core, 2
Clock tab (Date & Time Preference pane), 146
cloning utilities, 18
ColorSync utility, 177
Column View (Finder), 63
compressing files and folders, 68
Console utility, 178
Control key (^), ix
controls, standard window controls, 79
cookies, controlling, 170
Cover Flow View (Finder), 63

D

Dashboard, 84, 160
    adding and removing widgets, 87
    creating your own widgets, 88
    getting more widgets, 88
    personalizing widgets, 87
data migration, 24–29
    fine tuning, 27
Date & Time Preference pane, 146
Delete key, ix
desktop, 53
    adding URLs to, 171
    Show View Options, 53

Desktop folder, 36
Desktop Preference pane, 118
DEVICES (Finder sidebar), 58
diacritic accent mark keyboard shortcuts, 202
Digital Color Meter, 178
disk repair programs, third party, 112
disk space, reduced for Snow Leopard, 6
Disk Utility, 16, 178
    duplicating optical disks, 68
    S.M.A.R.T. Status, 109
disks
    booting from, 112
    Burn button for Finder toolbar, 58
    ejecting, 67
    reformatting, 67
display problems, troubleshooting, 106
Displays Preference pane, 129
Dock, 69–78
    adding items to, 70
    Dashboard, 84
    Exposé, 71
    Finder and, 69
    menu to configure options, 44
    menus, 72
    Preferences, 78
    removing items from, 71
    Trash, 75

upgrade in Snow Leopard,
    viii
Dock Preference pane, 121
Documents folder, 36
Downloads folder, 36
drives
    ejecting, 67
    noises in hard drive,
        troubleshooting,
        109
DVD Player, 161
DVDs
    CDs and DVDs Preference
        pane, 129
    duplicating, 68
    sharing, 142

E

Edit menu, 49
Eject button, ix
ejecting a drive or disk, 67
email
    Address Book application,
        158
    Mail & Chat tab in
        Parental Controls,
        149
    Mail application, 164
    upgrading from older Mac,
        29
Energy Saver Preference pane,
    130
erasing hard disk with Disk
    Utility, 16
Essential System Software
    option, 20
Exposé, 71, 94
    key commands, 95

Exposé and Spaces Preference
    pane, 122

F

Fan View (Stack), 73
Fast User Switching, 40
    enabling, 146
Fax tab (Print & Fax
    Preference pane), 138
File menu, 48
files and folders, 81
    Burn folders, 82
    compressing, 68
    copying files to new
        location on a disk,
        66
    creating folders, 65
    duplicating, 66
    file sharing, 143
    making alias for, 65
    managing file info with
        Spotlight, 91
    migrating from another
        Mac, 25
    regular folders, 81
    renaming, 64
    Smart folders, 83
Finder, 54–68
    Application menu, 46
    common tasks, 64
    customizing the toolbar,
        57
    Dock and, 69
    enhancements under Snow
        Leopard, 7
    not responding, 102
    Preferences, 59
    sidebar, 58

standard window, 55
    components of, 55
    views, 61
FireVault tab (Security
        Preference pane), 126
Firewall tab (Security
        Preference pane), 127
FireWire Target Disk Mode,
        26
Font Book, 162
fonts, Additional Fonts
        option, 21
Force Quit, 45
    ending unresponsive
            application, 100
    using on greedy processes,
            103
    using on unresponsive
            Finder, 102
Front Row, 162

G

Gamma settings, default
        correction, 12
GCD (Grand Central
        Dispatch), 2
General preferences (Finder),
        60
General tab (Security
        Preference pane), 125
Get Info button for Finder
        toolbar, 58
Get Info window, 91
Grab screen capture utility,
        179
Grand Central Dispatch
        (GCD), 2
Grapher, 179

Graphics Processing Unit
        (GPU), 4
Grid View (Stack), 73
Group accounts, 34
Guest accounts, 34

H

Help menu, 49
Hide ApplicationName menu
        entry, 47
Hide Others (Application
        menu), 47
Home folder, 35
    list of standard subfolders,
            35

I

iCal, 162
iChat, 163
    enhancements, viii, 8
    Parental Controls on, 149
Icon View (Finder), 61
iDisk, 187
iDisk tab (MobileMe
        Preference pane), 141
Image Capture, 163
IMAP (Internet Mail Access
        Protocol), 165
Info window, 91
infrared receivers, disabling
        remote control of, 126
installation, 13–23
    beginning, 20
    customizing for Snow
            Leopard, 20
    Macs compatible with
            Snow Leopard, 13

moving data and applications from another Mac, 24
    fine tuning data migration, 27
post-install tasks, 22
preparing to install Snow Leopard, 15
    preparing the hard disk, 16
Intel processors, 1
Internet Sharing option, 145
iPhoto
    Pictures folder, 37
    using pictures for screen saver, 119
iSync, 163
iTunes, 164

J

Java Preferences, 179
JavaScript, speediness under Snow Leopard, 5

K

key commands, 196
    common keyboard shortcuts, 197
    customizing, 202
Keyboard Preference pane, 132
    Keyboard Shortcuts tab, 133
    Keyboard tab, 133
Keyboard tab (Universal Access), 153
Keychain Access, 180
    menu extra for, 193

recovering forgotten password, 190
Secure Notes, 192
testing strength of passwords, 191
Keychain menu extra, 50
killing a program, 100

L

Labels preference (Finder), 60
Language & Text Preference pane, 123
Language Translations option, 21
Library folder, 36
List View (Finder), 62
List View (Stack), 74
logging in, 40
    Accounts Preference pane options for, 145
    disabling automatic login, 125
    remote login, 144
logging out, 40
    forcing after period of inactivity, 125
    key commands, 41
    Log Out Apple menu item, 45
logs for Mac OS X, 178

M

Mac information (About this Mac), 43
Mac OS X, vii
Mac OS X Software menu, 44
MacBook

Energy Saver Preference pane, 130
Trackpad Preference pane, 136
MacBook Air, data migration and, 26
Macs compatible with Snow Leopard, 13
Mail, 164
adding new accounts, 165
adding signature to outgoing mail, 165
deleting junk mail quickly, 166
junk mail filtering, 166
managing mailboxes, 166
searching, 166
Mail & Chat tab (Parental Controls), 149
Managed with Parental Controls accounts, 33
memory (RAM) module, defective, 108
menu bar, 42–53
Accounts menu, 52
Apple menu, 43
Application menu, 46
contents of, 42
keyboard shortcuts for items, 52
menu extras, 50
standard application menus, 48
menu extras, 50
for Keychain Access, 193
menu symbols, ix
metadata, 89
microphones, 140

Microsoft Exchange, 4
Migration Assistant, 24, 180
fine tuning data migration, 27
MobileMe, 183–188
adding or removing computers, 187
Back to My Mac, 185
clearing sync slate, 187
iDisk, 187
MobileMe account, 23
MobileMe Preference pane, 140
Account tab, 140
Back to My Mac tab, 142
iDisk tab, 141
Sync tab, 141
Mouse Preference pane, 134
Mighty Mouse options, 135
using non-Apple mouse, 135
Mouse tab (Universal Access), 154
Movies folder, 37
multiple processing core chips, 2
Music folder, 37

N

Network Preference pane, 142
network setup, 23
Network Utility, 180

O

OpenCL, 4
Option key, 203

Option symbol, ix

P

PAE (Physical Address
    Extension) of Intel
    chips, 15
Parental Controls, 33
Parental Controls Preference
    pane, 147
    Content tab, 148
    Logs tab, 149
    Mail & Chat tab, 149
    System tab, 147
    Time Limits tab, 149
partitioning your hard disk,
    18
password management, 190
    recovering forgotten
        password, 190
    strong passwords, 191
password, requiring for
    System Preferences
    panes, 125
Path button, adding to Finder
    toolbar, 57
Photo Booth, 167
Physical Address Extension
    (PAE) of Intel chips, 15
Pictures folder, 37
PLACES (Finder sidebar), 58
Places of Interest symbol, ix
Podcast Capture, 180
Power Adapter tab (Energy
    Saver Preference pane),
    130
power failure, automatic
    startup after, 131

PowerPC platform, removal of
    support for, 6
PowerPC-based Macs, 1
PRAM (parameter random
    access memory),
    resetting, 112
Preferences (Application
    menu), 46
Preferences (Dock), 78
Preferences (Finder), 59
Preview, 167
    enhancements, 9
Print & Fax Preference pane,
    137
printer sharing, 143
Printer Support option, 21
processes (greedy), Force
    Quitting, 103
Public folder, 37

Q

Quick Look (Finder), 65
QuickTime X, viii, 167
    enhancements, 10
Quit Application Name, 47

R

RAID Utility, 181
Recent Items menu, 44
reformatting disks, 67
Remote Apple Events option,
    145
Remote Install Mac OS X,
    181
Remote Login option, 144
Remote Management option,
    144
Restart Apple menu entry, 45

Rosetta, 6
Rosetta option, 22
RSS readers, 172
RSS Visualizer, 119

S

64-bit operating system, 3, 15
S.M.A.R.T. Status, 109
Safari, 168
    adding URL to desktop,
        171
    blocking pop-up ads, 170
    changing home page, 168
    controlling cookies, 170
    customizing toolbar, 172
    default RSS reader, 172
    deleting history, 170
    downloaded items
        location, 170
    enhancements, 5
    finding page not
        bookmarked, 169
    pages shown in Top Sites,
        169
    Private Browsing, 171
    remembering passwords
        for website logins,
        172
Safe Mode, booting in, 111
scanner sharing, 144
screen capture utility (Grab),
    179
screen reading utility
    (VoiceOver), 182
Screen Saver Preference pane,
    118
screen sharing, 143

MobileMe on remote Mac,
    186
SEARCH FOR (Finder
    sidebar), 59
Secure Notes, 192
security, 189–193
Security Preference pane, 124
    FireVault tab, 126
    Firewall tab, 127
Self-Monitoring, Analysis,
    and Reporting
    Technology
    (S.M.A.R.T.), 109
Services menu, 47
Set Up Bluetooth Keyboard
    option, 134
settings, migrating from
    another Mac, 25
Setup Assistant, 29
SHARED (Finder sidebar),
    58
Sharing Only accounts, 33
Sharing Preference pane, 142
    MobileMe Back to My
        Mac, 185
Show All (Application menu),
    47
shutting down, 40
    faster shutdown, 11
    key commands, 41
    scheduling automatic
        shutdown, 132
    Shut Down Apple menu
        entry, 45
sidebar (Finder), 58
    preferences for, 60
single user mode, 113
Sites folder, 38

sleeping, 41
  Energy Saver Preference
    pane options, 130
  Sleep Apple menu entry,
    45
Smart folders, 83
SMC (System Management
  Controller), 106
Snow Leopard
  64-bit applications, 3
  enhancements over Mac
    OS X, vii
  Macs compatible with, 13
  starting up, 38
Software Update application,
  44
Software Update Preference
  pane, 149
  Installed Software tab,
    150
  Scheduled Check tab, 149
Sound Preference pane, 138
  Input tab, 140
  Output tab, 139
  Sound Effects tab, 138
Spaces, 95
  configuring, 96
Spaces tab (Exposé and Spaces
  Preference pane), 122
speakers, 138
special characters, 202
  shortcuts on U.S. English
    keyboard, 203
Speech Preference pane, 150
  Speech Recognition tab,
    150
  Text to Speech tab, 151
Spotlight, 89

controlling indexing, 90
controlling ordering of
  results, 89
controlling results
  displayed, 89
file info, 91
key commands, 90
Spotlight Preference pane,
  128
Stack menu (Dock), 73
  view options, 73
Standard accounts, 33
starting up Snow Leopard, 38
  logging in, 40
  scheduling automatic
    startup, 132
  startup key commands, 39
Startup Disk Preference pane,
  152
startup problems,
  troubleshooting, 108
  hard drive making noises,
    109
  Mac beeps instead of
    starting, 108
  Mac not booting, 110
  resetting PRAM, 112
  using AppleJack, 113
Stickies, 172
swap files, security option for,
  126
System folder
  duplication of, 19
  migrating from another
    Mac, 25
system improvements in Snow
  Leopard, 11

System Management
        Controller (SMC), 106
System Preferences, 44, 115–
        154
    Accounts, 145
    Appearance, 118
    CDs and DVDs, 129
    Date & Time, 146
    Desktop and Screen Saver,
        118
    Displays, 129
    Dock, 121
    Energy Saver, 130
    Exposé and Spaces, 122
    Keyboard, 132
    Language and Text, 123
    MobileMe, 140
        Back to My Mac, 185
        Sync, 188
    Mouse, 134
    Network, 142
    non-Apple preference
        panes, 154
    Parental Controls, 147
    preference panes, 117
    Print and Fax, 137
    searching for preferences,
        116
    Security, 124
    Sharing, 142
    Software Update, 149
    Sound, 138
    Speech, 150
    Spotlight, 128
    Startup Disk, 152
    Time Machine, 152
    Trackpad, 136
    Universal Access, 152

System Profiler, 181
    Power section, 104

T

Terminal, 181
    split pane, in Snow
        Leopard, 12
Text tab (Language & Text
        Preference pane), 123
Text to Speech tab (Speech
        Preference pane), 151
TextEdit, 173
third-party preference panes,
        154
Time Limits tab (Parental
        Controls), 149
Time Machine, 174
Time Machine backup, data
        migration from, 27
Time Machine Preference
        pane, 152
Time Zone tab (Date & Time
        Preference pane), 146
time, System Preferences, 146
Trackpad Preference pane,
        136
    multitouch trackpads, 136
    older trackpads, 136
Trash, 75
troubleshooting Mac OS X,
        99–113
    misbehaving applications,
        100
        battery problems, 104
        display problems, 106
        Finder not responding,
            102

Force Quitting greedy
processes, 103
unresponsive
application, 100
USB device problems,
103
startup problems, 108
hard drive making
noises, 109
Mac beeps instead of
starting, 108
Mac not booting, 110
resetting PRAM, 112
using AppleJack, 113

U

Universal Access Preference
pane, 152
Hearing tab, 153
Keyboard tab, 153
Mouse tab, 154
Seeing tab, 153
USB device problems, 103
user accounts, 32–38
Accounts Preference pane,
145
Home folder, 35
Mail, 164
migration from another
Mac, 24
setting up, 34
setting up for Snow
Leopard, 23
types in Mac OS X, 32
utilities included with Snow
Leopard, 175–182
Activity Monitor, 175
Airport, 175

AppleScript Editor, 176
Audio MIDI Setup, 176
Bluetooth File Exchange,
176
Boot Camp Assistant, 177
ColorSync, 177
Console, 178
Digital Color Meter, 178
Disk Utility, 178
Exposé, 179
Grab, 179
Grapher, 179
Java Preferences, 179
Keychain Access, 180
Migration Assistant, 180
Network Utility, 180
Podcast Capture, 180
RAID Utility, 181
Remote Install Mac OS X,
181
System Profiler, 181
Terminal, 181
VoiceOver, 182
X11, 182
utilities, migrating from
another Mac, 25

V

VoiceOver screen reading
utility, 153, 182
volume, Sound Preference
pane, 138

W

wake up, faster, 11
web page for this book, xi
Web Sharing option, 144

Website Restrictions
(Parental Controls),
148
widgets (Dashboard), 84
adding and removing, 87
creating your own, 88
getting more, 88
personalizing, 87
window controls, 79
keyboard shortcuts, 80
Window menu, 49
Windows systems, MobileMe
on, 184
wireless network logon,
faster, 11

X
X11, 182
X11 option, 21
Xgrid Sharing option, 145

Get even more for your money.

Join the O'Reilly Community, and register the O'Reilly books you own. It's free, and you'll get:

- 40% upgrade offer on O'Reilly books
- Membership discounts on books and events
- Free lifetime updates to electronic formats of books
- Multiple ebook formats, DRM FREE
- Participation in the O'Reilly community
- Newsletters
- Account management
- 100% Satisfaction Guarantee

Registering your books is easy:

1. Go to: oreilly.com/go/register
2. Create an O'Reilly login.
3. Provide your address.
4. Register your books.

Note: English-language books only

To order books online:
oreilly.com/order_new

For questions about products or an order:
orders@oreilly.com

To sign up to get topic-specific email announcements and/or news about upcoming books, conferences, special offers, and new technologies:
elists@oreilly.com

For technical questions about book content:
booktech@oreilly.com

To submit new book proposals to our editors:
proposals@oreilly.com

Many O'Reilly books are available in PDF and several ebook formats. For more information:
oreilly.com/ebooks

O'REILLY®

Spreading the knowledge of innovators   oreilly.com

Buy this book and get access to the online edition for 45 days—for free!

Mac OS X Snow Leopard Pocket Guide
By Chris Seibold
September 2009, $14.99
ISBN 9780596802721

With Safari Books Online, you can:

Access the contents of thousands of technology and business books

- Quickly search over 7000 books and certification guides
- Download whole books or chapters in PDF format, at no extra cost, to print or read on the go
- Copy and paste code
- Save up to 35% on O'Reilly print books
- **New!** Access mobile-friendly books directly from cell phones and mobile devices

Stay up-to-date on emerging topics before the books are published

- Get on-demand access to evolving manuscripts.
- Interact directly with authors of upcoming books

Explore thousands of hours of video on technology and design topics

- Learn from expert video tutorials
- Watch and replay recorded conference sessions

O'REILLY®

Spreading the knowledge of innovators   oreilly.com